To MI
G

ICIe,
Thomas

God Bless u.

$\mathcal{F}$alse $\mathcal{L}$abels

Don't Let People Label You

13 uplifting short stories of Inspiration,
Hope, Encouragement and
Empowerment

MARIE-CLAIRE N KUJA

False Labels: Don't Let People Label You
Copyright © 2012 by Marie-Claire N Kuja

ISBN: 978-0-9850226-9-3

The new international reader's version
copyright(c)-1995, 1996, 1998 by Biblica, Inc.

The way (an illustrated edition of the living bible)
Copyright(c) 1971 by Tyndale house publishers.
Copyright(c) 1972 by youth for Christ international

Foreword by: Rev Perry Wooten
Senior Pastor of Eastchester
Presbyterian Church Bronx NY USA

Chief Editor: Mr Terry Berogan
Illustrated by: Mr Gary Sanchez
Edited by: Mr Atumo Daniel
Proofread by: Mr Emuobome M Amraibure

Book design by: Maureen Cutajar
www.gopublished.com

Dedication

This book is dedicated to:

My God: The King of all kings.

To my lovely parents: Your integrity, love, sacrifice, humility and compassion have left an incredible impression in my life. I will forever be grateful to both of you.

To my Big Brother (Ni Adolf): When God gave you to me, He gave me gold. Your unconditional love and sacrifice for me means the world.

To Nunichu and Wagala: My two precious treasures. Being your mother is the greatest reward I ever had. You bring me more joy than I could ever hope for.

And to all the kujaS: Ma Bea, Ni Divine, Ma Rachel, Kabi, Anna, Ga, & kah & my cousin Ma Commy: Your love, encouragement and support are second to none. Our greatest days are still ahead.

Acknowledgements

As with any project, it takes a great team to make all the elements come together in a book. I want to extend my personal and humble gratitude to:

God – Who gave me the inspiration, who created me so uniquely, who has given me lots of chances in life, who made me know that He specializes in the impossibilities, and can take a person like me, a stained –sin soul and make something out of. Who made me know I could look beyond Any False Labels.

Mom and Dad – To whom I have drawn so much inspiration from. Thank you so much for the strong foundation you laid for us. Thank you for introducing me to this Great King, The God of all gods.

Adolf Kuja [My big Brother] – Who has believed so much in me and has given me unconditional support throughout my whole life and with this book project. I love and thank you endlessly.

Mr. Terry Berogan–My editor – Thanks a billion for not only editing this book as a professional but as a father correcting her daughter's work. Thank you for the heart and passion you put into the work.

Atumo Daniel – I thank you very immensely for your enthusiasm, excitement, and for the time you took to read, edit and write such a beautiful review. Thank you moreover for believing in the success of this book.

Gary Sanchez – My illustrator for the beautiful artwork. They were so well done. Thanks Gary.

Clement Okpor – Your godly wisdom and unique insights have made this book a great success. I thank you.

Michael Amraibure [My boo] – I thank you from the bottom of my heart for all your contributions and Inspirations and for all the sleepless nights you spent proof-reading or editing or doing something for this project to be successful. Thank you.

To all the Kuja's and my one and only cousin Fokumlah Comfort – For all your sacrifices and unconditional love expressed to me over the years, I love and thank you.

Allied girls – Fatima Mansaray, Nana Akyaa kwarteng, Olabisi Deen Kamara, Titilope Akinde, Latifa Monsunmola Folly, Kerry Walker, Shermain, Jamaine, Thanya Dorose, Joujou Charles, Mabel, Rita, Patience and everyone from the class of 2010. All your moral support and the beautiful friendship makes life interesting.

To Chichi Onukwue, Amabel Ngwasha, & Mariama Akrah, your friendship is precious. Thank you.

Rev. Perry Wooten – Senior Pastor of the Eastchester Presbyterian Church Bronx New York for the beautiful foreword and encouragements. For everything you have done for me over the years, I thank you immensely.

Sister Etta Graham-Mitchell and brother Jonas Attuh-Mensah of the Eastchester Presbyterian Church Bronx New York for taking time out of your very busy schedule to review the manuscript. Thank you so much for all the feedback and beautiful reviews. I really appreciate it.

Joana Penn of Thecreativepenn and Dale Beaumont of GetPublishTV.com, both of whom I have learn a lot from their online teachings. I have learned more than I can explain from you guys and I thank you.

Contents

Foreword

"Why?"

That is the most common and most frequently asked question by men, women and children. As children we ask "Why must I do that?" As adults we inquire, "Why is life like that?" As thinkers we search the greatest unknowns of all: "Why the world is 'constructed' this way?" "How do those stars hang there in space?" "Why do things happen the way they do?"

There are many, many other questions we can and do ask, of course. Some revolve around the creation of the universe, some are motivated by human behavior, and a few are centered in the incomplete knowledge of every human being.

Many of the 'why's' we ask are important and crucial and for the most part reflect our background, education and interests. But there is one 'why' that overshadows every other 'why,' and that is the 'why' of our existence.

Marie-Claire does a masterful job in addressing this issue. Importantly, she does it in a way which is neither as a professor who pretends to have all the answers or as a paragon of experience who seeks to overpower the reader with the breadth and variety of her exposure to all forms of human endeavor.

Rather, Marie-Claire seeks to guide the reader along a path which is familiar and inviting, safe yet challenging.

Specifically, she does what every sound, mature person of faith must do. She encourages us to "Trust in the Lord with all your heart and lean not on your own understanding. And He will make your paths straight." (Proverbs 3:5)

As an intelligent and faithful servant of the living GOD, she recognizes early on that we cannot find ourselves if we run from the Source of all life. She reminds us that we cannot determine our ultimate purpose in life if we ignore the ultimate purpose for which we were made. She continually calls us to remember that we cannot ignore GOD's call to serve and acknowledge the needs, hopes and ambitions of others and assume that we will find fulfillment in our individual efforts and struggles.

Another advantage of this book is that the author offers us a choice. We can be either "a doer or a one-to." That is, we can either take responsibility for where we are and what we are doing and what we are called to be, or we can continue to be tools of events and the instruments of the power that others seek to wield over us.

Whatever your frame of mind – downcast, used up or forward looking – this book is for you. Not only will those who feel useless be emboldened to start again, but those who are "on a roll" will gain new insights into the most rewarding purpose and the direction of their efforts.

Benjamin Franklin said, "If you love life then don't waste time, for that is the stuff of which it is made." I would encourage every intelligent and faithful reader to spend your time wisely – by reading and absorbing the lessons of this excellent testimony of truth.

Rev. Perry Wooten,
Senior pastor of Eastchester Presbyterian church,
Bronx N Y U.S.A

Introduction

Two images from my childhood come rushing to mind when I think about the person I am today and why I do what I want to do. Why am I drawn to sharing my story with people all over the world?

The first image was from the first time I was treated like an outcast and told by many that I will never amount to anything. Having a child as a teenager and out of wedlock is wrong but not as bad as to earn me the names I earned. The second image was from the way my son was treated. Not only did people call me useless for having a child out of wedlock, they transferred that unto to him and called him a bastard. That was so hurtful and destroying emotionally and completely damaged everything I ever had as self-worth.

Every time that I heard people call my son and I names, it reminded me of what I was not. During that period in my life I was uncomfortable, insecure and struggling. I was at war with myself .But one day, so tired of fighting with myself I decided to turn things the other way. I was determined to know why I was created and what my purpose in life is. While on a quest on finding out my purpose I started researching the Bible and other inspirational books. Then I started praying even more. I also started writing to myself (a journal). Gradually I noticed my journal was becoming a journey, not just a simple destination. They were real life happening at the moment. I'd completed two to three a week. They were thick and full and ripe with feelings and thoughts. Whenever I was down and read from my journals I felt like an angel was talking to me. It felt so uplifting. My own words became an inspiration to me. I was reminded of how important it is to believe in myself and remember that we are all created unique and special. During this time while I was praying and asking God to make it clear to me why I was on earth, I came to this wonderful self realization. I realized I am a masterpiece carefully handpicked by God. I am not a mistake, nor useless nor a failure, nor any of the other names I was called. I also realized I had to be myself. Then I decided to do what I am asking you today to do. To take off those old false labels and re-label yourself with what God says about you. He made you special and unique

People around me would read them and said: "Oh! I totally felt this way or I relate so much—". I was fascinated with people's truth, how they were perceived by others and how that didn't necessarily jibe with what they felt. People would say: "you are so put together" but didn't know what a struggle my life was. They also didn't know how apart I was from myself. I wish there was a book like this when I was growing up. I had so many different struggles centered around negative belief system I had formed based on what other people said about me. This is a universal struggle, "I was bullied and called so many names as a teen which left a very lasting scar in my life", said a school friend who had read my journal. Then I knew I was not alone. But how can we combat this? How can we empower our minds and spirits and the generation to come?

So the idea of having a strong voice became very confronting.

People all have edges but the challenge is not to hide from them. I made a pact to share my story with others because I believe only shared experiences help.

However, if we don't know any better we would wear these false labels like they are truths, limiting us from what God has in store for us. Yet lots of people have heeded to these false labels and have ended on the side lines of life, feeling washed out and drowning in self-pity and low self esteem. False labels have caused lots of people their lives by way of drugs, prostitution, alcoholism and even death.

How do you break out and experience the full potential that God has in store for you? I will challenge you in the pages of **False Labels** to break out of a barely get-by-life style and live your life to the fullest, celebrating your uniqueness every day. Stop going through life with self pity and low self esteem, focusing on all the negative things and feeling inadequate always dwelling on one thing or the other. Remember people can only call you the names you answer to… Life has a divine purpose and meaning. Don't sit on the other side of life and let others steal your joy. Don't let life pass you by.

False Labels therefore comes as a counteract to derogatory labels .Each story is carefully and uniquely written to inform, educate, empower, inspire, and redirect people both young and old. The stories all end with some words to ponder and a prayer. Some of them have images for better understanding. The central message to the reader is that they are not a write off. The book is meant to tell people what they can do through Christ rather than what they can't do. It's also intended to give people a push and help them win at life and regain their lost hope and most importantly learn how to celebrate their uniqueness.

Proverbs 18:4 says, "Your words are like life-giving water." There are people in need of life-giving water, who are lonely and hurting; they've been through disappointments, suffering, heartache and pain. God has given us something to offer them - our words; which can bring healing; lift others out of depression by way of encouragement and compliments. We can help set people free from the strongholds that are keeping them back.

And by so doing they will be able to live a purpose driven life while making their lives count for Christ. Look beyond false labels.

Story #1

"Just Who Are You & What Is Your Lists?"

"Girl! Wait till you see my ride. I'm gonna be gaming it in all kinds of rides," says one of the girls in my obstetric (OB) class as we sat down for a talk.

When I was in nursing school, I met some of the most amazing friends of my life. One day during our break, while we were chatting with each other, something came up about what we will be doing after nursing school and what we think our purpose in life is. We all have different perspectives on life and following are some of my friends' responses.

One said, "Oh my husband and I have already started building a clinic. I intend to go back home to Liberia and open a clinic so I can help others. There are many women and children in my country suffering. I wish I can be of help one day by God's grace."

Another responded with, "I'm working on starting a foundation in my country to help women and children in need. My country has suffered so much from war. I hope one day I will be able to provide some kind of help to them, especially children orphaned by AIDS."

Another friend said, "I will travel the world and enjoy my life to the fullest." She also added, "How I love nice clothes and shoes. I will buy the most beautiful home and probably live my life with my husband if any one comes my way."

And yet another said, "Girl, my ride? You will need to come see what I will be cruising in." From all the responses, you can clearly see that everyone has a different perspective on life.

And the last of my friends said, "Guys, with this suffering, I will not give a dime to anyone because no one cares about me right now anyway."

I thought all the answers were interesting and different.

MY TAKE

What I think is my purpose in life can be completely different from others thinking because after all God created all of us very differently and uniquely and also planted different gifts and talents in us.

But you see a whole 60-70% of us will go to our graves without knowing who we are, why we were created in the first place and worst of all why God gave us all these great gifts and talents and opportunities. I believe very strongly that we are not on earth by accident but because He meant for us to be here. I also believe that He made everyone with very special gifts, skills, abilities and talents for a reason.

> *It is God himself who has made us what we are and has given us new lives from Christ Jesus, and long ages ago He planned that we should spend these lives in helping others.*
> **Ephesians 2:10**

But more often than not, we just settle into living our daily routines of waking up in the morning, eating, going to work (in jobs we sometimes don't like), coming back home, eating, taking a shower and going to sleep to get ready for the next day. While we are going in circles with this routine, minutes, hours, days, weeks, months and years go by and, because time waits for no one, we get old and die. Most people have the opportunities of knowing their purpose when they are young, but ignore or do not recognize these opportunities because life is so sweet or bitter that it deters their minds.

> *The Truth Is That Only You Can Be You And Only You Can Choose To Surrender Your Life Completely To God.*
> **Erik Rees**

The best way to thrive in today's world is living a purpose-driven life. A life that is meaningful. A life where you are following your own values and not anyone else's, where you surrender all you have to God to expand His glory. I am as guilty here as anyone because I lived a very confused life for quite a while and a lot of things happened to me, as it can to all of us, that completely deterred my ways of thinking and looking at things. But somewhere deep inside me, there was a void. I wished that I was doing something else instead of cleaning people's houses or working in retail stores. I knew very well I was wasting that precious time we have in life but did not know what to do. I had my youngest son in September 2004 and instead of celebrating I was suffering from the worst form of postpartum depression. It got so bad I had to beg my mother to come from Africa and take the poor little baby with her and let me face the challenges on my own. It was as though everything that happened to me from my childhood to now came pressing down on me. And, as if that was not enough, I had no job, no friends nor any family here. I was literally breaking down. But one evening in November 2005, a certain journalist hosted a show for women who have gone through all kinds of lows and adversities which caused them to lose their identities and self worth. Amongst the many women present were those who lost their husbands through divorce or whose husbands left them for other women, these women were labeled by friends or loved ones as dirty or unworthy. Like: "Oh, you are too fat," or "You don't have what it takes so you can't do it," or "You cannot amount to anything." These labels, whether false or true, hurt people and give them little or no confidence and self worth and they have to live with them for a life time or until they can get help.

The journalist's closing remarks and advice to these ladies and hundreds of others with problems, was that: while you are lying there on the couch (and I was lying on the couch) beating up yourself about something someone did to you, first ask, "Why was I created and why am I here, what is my purpose, why did God create me? Am I here to live my own life or please others? Was I created to serve God or man? Am I here for others to define the course of my life?" This was a huge wake up call for me. It reminded me of the words I heard many years ago at my dad's sermon in which he had given each member of the church some cards on which was printed, **"Who you are makes a difference, so make your life count."** This journalist's advice to the women and my dad's words echoed in my mind. I laid there on the couch and kept repeating those words. If I were gone today, who would say I made an impact in their lives? Was I really making my life count, if all I had known was live in bitterness and regrets? What legacy was I going to leave while I am gone? It was a very scary moment because then I started to realize what a waste my life had been. That also reminded me of a sermon I heard from my pastor in which he said that our time on earth is like that little dash we see in cemeteries, from the date of birth to the date of death. And I also remembered these words...

I am only one
But still I am one
I cannot do everything
But still I can do something
And because I cannot do everything
I will not refuse to do that which I can do...

Hellen Keller

The truth is that you and I each have only one life to live here on earth. And that little time we have is fleeting. It's running and does not wait for anyone.

Teach us to number our days and recognize how few they are; help us to spend them as we should. **Psalms 90:12**

If you use what you have to impact a thousand people Or even just one person that is still well done. **Erik Rees**

As I laid there and continued to ask myself these questions and continued to reflect on my life, my writing was born. After the show, I went to my room with a notebook and a pen to see if I could come up with my purpose in life. I started by researching my Bible, starting from the beginning with the creation. But nothing inspired me, so what I believed was most important was asking God and letting Him direct me towards what my purpose was. I thought about what really mattered in life and would I have made a difference when I am gone. I realized that nothing mattered unless I decided to start making my life meaningful instead of just drifting through life without purpose and without caring. What will I do with my life? Will I consume it? Cruise through it or use it in a way that will glorify God? The questions were just endless and from then on I was willing to let God use my one and only life to make it useful for Him. I decided to make a complete U–Turn and let God in my life, helping me to decide what was important to me, which was not very funny? It was like an x-ray that scans pictures of your inner- most self and shows it to you. Like it was intended to, it took pictures on where I was in life and put it right back in my face so I could see where I was in life. And truly I was not in a good place, I was living in fear, anger, unhappiness, hopelessness and so on. And when I started to practice making that life changing turn, other things started changing as well.

The great news is that YOU matter, you matter to yourself, to those around you, and to God. How do you plan to make your life count? Do you want to continue drifting through life, or do you want to make a complete turn around and let God use you for His glory? The diagram of the U-Turn below will assist you a great deal because it actually shows you where you are now and where you are heading in your life.

I have been trying to do those things I believe make me happy as well as serve God. The more I lose myself in helping someone, the happier I get. It is the most rewarding feeling when you know why you are here instead of drifting through life in confusion. One of the things I like to do is giving, talking and working for women and children. I have been doing just that to the best of my ability since I made that decision to turn my life around and my life is renewed. He created us with all these gifts and talents for a purpose. He wants us to use these gifts and talents to help others, to spread the spirit of God to the souls of others. What is your purpose? Let's find out what it is and serve God with what He blessed us with, whether we are young and strong or older. What does your heart desire? There is something deep in your heart which God has planted there. All of us are called and equipped to do something to help God's children.

It is possible to give away and become richer! It is possible to hold on too tightly and lose everything. Yes the liberal man shall be rich! By watering others, he waters himself. **Proverbs 11:24, 25.**

THE U-TURN

Ignorant me
Do I want to
continue in darkness?
Darkness, anger, fear,
bitterness,
Emptiness, sadness,
troubled, lost,
frustration

Who I am matters;
I will make my
life meaningful.
Am I living the life
that counts? A life
that glorifies God?
Am I a vessel of God's love?
Living a purpose driven life, focus,
contribution, Impacting other
people's lives with my god given gifts.
Being a blessing to others.
Be at peace with myself,

Readiness to
be submissive
to Christ
Am I ready to
surrender all to God?
A life of meaning,
hope, happiness,
peace of mind,
gratitude.

Readiness to serve.
Am I ready and willing to
use my life to empower
others? Am I ready to
unwrap my package?
Dreams, choices, direction,
mission, Balance, vision

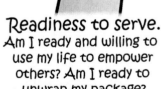

A messenger for Christ
Am I ready to go where He sends me?
Talents, skills, abilities, knowledge,
heart's desires, Experiences.

In 100% of the time, it takes boldness to ignore what people think or say about you and follow your heart. It is of course not very easy to have visions and dreams ignored because they will constantly be there waiting for you.

Be bold, be brave and take a step of faith towards making your life count lest God will think we rob Him. **Malachi 3:8 will a man rob God?**

Following your heart is living a purpose driven life of obeying God, which simplifies your life. And, by so doing you feel happier and peaceful within your soul.

The Word

We are who we are because He is love
We are who we are because His Mercies brightens
We are who we are because He is love
We are who we are because He created us for a purpose,
We are who we are because He is kind.

I realize I am a masterpiece handpicked by God. I will live with confidence, knowing that I am valuable in His eyes and have something great to offer my family, my society and the world.

I believe God made me exactly the way He wanted, and He equipped me with everything I need to live an abundant, fulfilled life.

*I will keep stretching, growing and learning and not allow fear
or insecurities to hold me back. I will tap into everything God
had planned in me.*

One of the greatest ways to share Jesus with those in your
world is to use those given gifts you have in your box, it's
to use what you have in your hand, and unwrap the gifts
He gave you and share them with others.

If you have been given the spiritual gift of encouragement, then be encouraging to the people in your life. There
are people around you who are down and just need a kind
word from someone to get them going. Reach out to them.
If you have the gift of hospitality, think of ways to open up
your home to help someone in need to deepen
relationships. Maybe there is a really painful experience in
your life that God helped you through that can give you a
special insight to help others with a similar problem. I was a
teenage mother. Wrong, yes! I was given all kinds of labels
like, "She will never amount to anything. She is a second
hand girl, a rejected cargo and so on." But, God's label for
me was and is to have a rewarding and prosperous life and
not the life people thought or said I was going to have. I
was given a second chance. In the same way, I am turning
my scars into stars by using my experience to help other
young girls who find themselves in this place I once was. I
want to tell them to throw away those old lies that are said
about them, those old labels given to them by those who
know not the love of God, and wear God's label proudly
saying "I am a child of God."

All of us have something that can help change another's
life in one way or the other. God is not asking you to stand
on street corners and shout "Jesus Loves You" to those

walking by, but he does ask us to be ready to give an account of the hope and love we do have for His children.

Spend today thinking of a few steps you could take to start delivering the Good News to those in your world. Think of those times you have had deep problems and God helped you through someone else. You can do the same for others. You can be a smile giver, the giver of God's love and help.

Be a messenger today for God! Be a useful vessel!

God gives
To us the gift of
Time to use as best we can
To live each moment in His will
According to his plan, life is short, live for God
a purpose driven life.

What is in our hands? In a sense, our lives are in our hands. We choose whether we'll squander the hours, the days, the weeks, the months, and years in our own pursuits or if we'll live an obedient life that's useful to Almighty God by serving others, His children. We will be surprised what He can do through us if we obediently do what he asks.

What is in your hands?

Prayer

O that my life may
Useful be as I serve you faithfully
And may the world see Christ in me
This is my honest prayer,
Amen!

Story #2

Impacts of Bullying

Dona was a girl who was bullied all through high school for being geeky, fat and short. She was called "the thing." Surprisingly, she continued to feel the same way even throughout her first year in college. She began to believe what her name callers had told her, she was the "thing." Those derogatory words just stuck. She had no self esteem or self worth and had thought of taking her life many times because she had no friends. Those words were so ironed in her mind that even when someone complimented her as being pretty, she dismissed it because she thought that was another way of mocking her or maybe they just pitied her. She was so depressed that she started isolating herself from everyone. But one day while she was watching television, she saw reports of another teen that was teased in the same manner and decided to take his life. She immediately related to his experience. When she heard what those kinds of feelings could do to someone, she began to talk to people about the way she was feeling and started seeking help. She got advice and support from her school chaplain and her teachers and her life has never been the same. The way she was looking at her appearance and self esteem changed. She began to view herself as worthy and important. She began to feel like God loved her.

What Dona did was stand up for herself and fight against her name callers. Her bravery and courage to talk about it to someone saved her life. She refused to continue to sit around in self pity and let what people thought of her steal her joy and determine the course of her beautiful life.

On the other hand, there are teenagers like Dona who do not have the courage on their own to talk to people about being bullied. They tend to keep to themselves because of the abuse they experience. Some of these teenagers commit suicide as a result, while a hand full of others carry these thoughts into their adulthood. One example is the case of Kam whom I met at my job many years ago.

She was the biggest complainer of all times. Despite coming from the same continent (Africa) with me and living here in the U.S, working as a registered nurse, she still did not see anything good in herself. Kam complained about her whole appearance, including the way her eyes, ears, nose, buttocks, breast and legs looked. She was never happy with anything. Her complaining became a habit and everyone on the unit knew her for that trait. She even called herself names like,

I am so stupid,
I am so fat,
I can never do anything right.
Nobody cares about me.

Everyone else just assumed that was who she was and went with the flow, but I thought there was more to it. Kam was my boss making it very difficult to ask her why she was so hard on herself despite all the blessings I saw around her. She was married to a very handsome and rich man who treated her like a queen. She was a mother of four beautiful kids; she had a good car and a beautiful home. Physically she was good looking and yet she was consumed with self-pity. She had no self esteem, no faith nor confidence. As it so happened, we were stuck together for almost three years which is enough time to be able to get to know the people you work with because it becomes like your second home and family. After some time had passed Kam eventually opened up to some of us co-workers. What I found out about Kam was shocking to me. She had a very difficult childhood. She was bullied for being overweight while growing up and never fit in as a teenager. She was teased and called all sorts of names from fat, chubby and short. Back in her school days whenever there was a school activity and she wanted to participate, she was bullied and laughed at and told she was too fat to do anything. She had also said her biggest challenge came from home where she was the only fat and short kid in the family and was teased even by all of her family.

It is amazing how words can have a very lasting impact

The abusive name calling affected her so much even into her adult life, into her marriage, her job, and her day to day living. She became extremely withdrawn and isolated. She got married early in high school when she found a guy who loved her for who she was. Kam said even though she found a husband and he did everything to make her happy, she was completely in her own world still living with the past abuses. She had never been able to forgive those in her past who verbally abused her. She still held on to the entire name calling and teasing from her school and family. She also was bothered by the fact that even her immediate family did not support her. All they did was put her down.

Her situation was so sad that I thought, "Yes that is bullying of the first class" just like what I faced when I was growing up. Kam without knowing any better became a self-bully, imposing false labels on herself and sabotaging her own well being. I could relate to her in a lot of ways. I had once been in her position and complained and blamed everyone around me for my setbacks. She was definitely not alone.

The difference between Kam's story and mine was that, in my situation I was blessed to have a mother who quickly stepped in and stopped me from sinking into self-pity and pain. My mother told me that in life everyone needs to take full responsibility for all their actions and stop blaming others around them. She had used a lot of practical life lessons to teach me but the one that has stuck with me till this day is the story of David and Goliath. She told me the story when I was younger and it did not mean so much to me because I did not understand the importance and how it should affect me. But when I left my family and was in the world on my own, I had to face all kinds of challenges where her lessons have been very useful and have continued to shape my path till this day.

DAVID & GOLIATH

1 Samuel Chapter 16
Samuel Anoints David, the youngest son of Jesse to be
king of Israel

1 Samuel Chapter 17
David kills Goliath

In the story of David and Goliath, we were told how
David, a small young Israelite, won the fight against
Goliath, the giant Philistine, with a sling and a stone.

Taking a step back to 1 Samuel chapter 17, The
Philistines gathered their army together for war. They
came to Socoh in Judah, and set up their camp at Ephes
and Azekah. Saul and the armies of Israel gathered
together and camped in the valley of Elah lining up their
men to fight the Philistines. The Philistine army was
camped on the hill on one side of the valley while Israel
was on the other side with the valley between them.

In verse 4 a mighty hero named Goliath came out of the
Philistines camp and challenged anyone from the Israelites to
battle him. Goliath was from Gath and was more than nine
feet tall. He had a bronze helmet on his head and wore a coat
of bronze armor. He wore bronze leg guards, carried a
bronze javelin on his back and a spear as big as a weaver's
rod. Its iron point weighed 15 pounds. The man who carried
his shield walked along in the front of him.

Verses 8, 9 &10 said Goliath stood and shouted to the
soldiers of the Israel saying, "Why do you have to come
out and line up for battle? I'm Philistine. You are servants
of Saul. Choose one of your men and have him come
down and face me. If he's able to fight and kill me we'll
become your slaves. But if I win and kill him you will

become our slaves and serve us." Goliath continued, "This very day I dare the soldiers of Israel to send a man down to fight against me."

Verse 11 goes on to say Saul and the whole army of Israel heard what the Philistines said. They were terrified and in verse 24 when Israel's army saw Goliath, all of them ran away from him, filled with fear.

Everyone else was afraid to face Goliath except David.

David said in verse 32 to Saul: "Don't let anyone lose hope because of the Philistines. I'll go out and fight him." But Saul was not sure about David because he was still young, while he himself had been a warrior since he was a boy.

In verses 34, 35 and 36 David said, "I have been taking care of my father's sheep and have protected our flocks from lions and bears devouring our sheep. I have saved many sheep from the lions and bears mouth. If it turned around to attack me, I would grab hold of its beard and strike it down and kill it. In fact I have killed both a lion and a bear. I will do the same to this philistine. He is not even circumcised.

He has dared the army of the living God.

The Lord saved me from the paw of the lion. He saved me from the paw of a bear. And he will save me from the powerful hand of this Philistine too."

At this point, Saul had confidence in David and told him, "Go, and may the Lord be with you". We are further told how Saul dressed David in his own military clothes, putting a coat of bronze armor on him and a bronze helmet on his head. David even put on Saul's own clothes over his. But after walking around in all of the armor, he was not used to wearing such heavy and restrictive armor, so he took it off.

In verse 40 David did the most amazing thing. David picked up his walking staff. He went down to the stream and chose five smooth stones. He put them in the pocket of his shepherd's bag, took his sling in his hand and approached Goliath. At the same time the Philistines kept coming closer to David. The man who was carrying Goliath's shield walked along in front of him. Goliath looked David over but saw how young he was. He saw a tanned and handsome young man and hated him right away. He said to him, "Why are you coming at me with sticks? Do you think I'm just a dog?" The Philistines called out curses to David in the name of his God. "Come over here," he said. "I'll feed your body to the birds of the air! I'll feed it to the wild animals!"

David said to Goliath, "You are coming to fight me with a sword, a spear and a javelin. But I 'm coming against you in the name of the Lord who rules over all. He's the one you have dared to fight."

David won the fight against Goliath with a sling and a stone in verse 50. He struck the Philistine down and killed him with a sling and a stone, without even using a sword.

In our day to day lives we are faced with giants who come in different forms and colors. They stalk us every minute. Sometimes you wake up hating to face the day because they have been with you all night. They are with you while you eat, while you work and in your most private moments. They are constantly reminding you of all your setbacks and disappointments throughout your life.

Goliath symbolizes some of the difficult day to day challenges we face such as:

Self Bullying
Self -sabotage
Work place bullying
Name calling

SELF-BULLYING

What is it that you constantly talk to yourself about? Do you say things like?

I am hopeless
I am stupid
I am an idiot
I can never do anything right
No one likes me?

If you do, give yourself a very serious knock on the head, because you are the one bullying yourself. You are the one sticking false labels on yourself and putting your own very self down. If you were walking down the street and see your brother or sister or even a friend being bullied, you will instinctively want to protect that person. So why then would you allow yourself to be bullied?

WORKPLACE-BULLYING

Bullying in the workplace is such a vicious cycle. Actually I call it a work place hazard. It could be a boss whom all he does is sabotage and criticize everything you do, or your co-workers ganging up against you because they are jealous, or it could be in the form racial discrimination. Bullying can also be in the form of rudeness, intimidation or verbal name calling. It is a psychological violence because it's very subjective and self damaging. Lots of lives both young and old have been lost by means of suicide and many homes destroyed as a result of bullying.

Whatever the case, just look at things differently. Remember who you belong to and who you serve. It should also be worth taking note that the people who bully you do so for lots of reasons. Some of which could be low self-esteem or lack of confidence on their part, or maybe they are intimidated by some trait you have that they wish they had, or their own insecurities. So they try to find a way to destroy someone else's life because by doing so they feel gratified. A lot has been said about bullying and how it occurs, and a lot more still needs to be told because it seems like an unending vicious cycle.

Bullying is primitive.

SELF-SABOTAGE

"I no longer look at every reflection of myself and see a map of disappointment. I see vigor, curves and force, an organic tumble of sensual, sexual energy. I stand straighter. I breathe deeper. My heart opens" **Lise Funderburg, writer**

We get so depressed and angry when people call us names or sabotage us or try to stick false labels on us. But what if you are the one sabotaging yourself? What if you are the one calling yourself names such as:

I am too short
I am too fat
I am too little
I am too tall
I am not worth anything
I wish I was like John or Mary
I don't like my nose
I cannot do anything good.
I am so unworthy I can't do that.

The one thing I know for sure is that there are no two versions of any human being, meaning there is only one you and you alone on the face of the earth. You don't have to try to be someone else but your own very self. You have to accept and appreciate who you are and how you were created.

We are told in 1 Sam chapter 17:40 that David went to the stream and picked five smooth stones. And it was just one amongst these five that took Goliath down once and for all. I want to encourage everyone who has been faced with any kind of Goliath in their lives to stand up in grand style. Stand up and fight against them just like David did.

But remember, not physically, but with faith, courage and confidence. David was very young and small in stature and Goliath was a giant. But because of the faith David had in the God he serves, he was able to conquer Goliath. I want us to face our Goliaths differently, peacefully and smart.

My mother told me this story because David was human and not any different from anyone else. He made a lot of mistakes, he may have sinned, but he never let the past or others put him down, neither did he heed to what people said about him. He was never discouraged. Goliath is a symbol representing the giants or difficulties one faces in life. If we follow David's example and ignore those false and negative voices that are out to discourage and degrade us, we will see all challenges as an opportunity, an opportunity to conquer all the obstacles that have for so long held us back, seeking the wisdom and the power of God.

In today's world there are lots of tools God has given us to be able to conquer those Goliaths we may face. There are such tools as faith, courage, confidence, boldness, self esteem and more. Prayer supersedes everything. But when we pray we need to have faith that God will help us fight our battles, or better still, help us win. In 1 Samuel 17:32-37 David's faith and courage were so obvious. He knew that if God had saved him from the paws of the lion and the bear, He would do the same by helping him bring down Goliath. In the same way, if we face our day to day Goliaths with the same attitude, what we think to be impossible will be nothing before God. Think about some of the battles you have won and the many good things God has done in your life. If He helped you the first time, He can do even more if we put our trust in Him and learn how to surrender our burdens to Him.

David's boldness also shows through when he decided to step up to fight Goliath when all his brothers were all stricken by fear of the giant (1 Sam 17:32). In verse 45 David was so bold, confident and faithful that he had no fear, no worries or self doubts.

If we will dare to trust God and face all our Goliaths like David did, God will help us win.

God's approval & not people David, Saul and brothers

So many people gain their sense of worth based on what others think of them.

Do they like me?
Do they approve of me?
Do they think I'm important?

Many people become something they are not because they think by conforming to the expectations of others they will get somewhere in life. It is very liberating when you realize that you don't need approval of others to be who you are or get where you want to be in life and fulfill your God-given destiny. All you need is approval from God. All you need is to have faith in yourself and God and believe in who He created you to be. It's time to live feeling secure, being the person God made you to be, not what someone else wants you to be. When you are secured in who God created you to be and confident enough in the destiny in front of you, then it doesn't matter what others say or do. Make pleasing and living for the Lord your number one priority. Not only will you live life in more freedom and happiness, but you will become everything God created you to be.

Instead of negative self-talk, change your thoughts and say good things about yourself. Use words and phrases that will help encourage you and build you up instead of putting you down. I truly believe in affirmations because they encourage and empower us. It's more like having your own cheering squad in word form. They have been used by great people to achieve tremendous goals. They are statements you want to believe in and hold on to. Words to say to yourself every time you get those negative self talks or thoughts or when someone tries put you down.

Remove the old labels and start re-labeling yourself with what God says about you.

You could make up your own affirmations by saying things like:

I am uniquely and specially made
I am worthy
I am lovable
I am beautiful
I am successful
I can achieve any dream I set my mind on
I am the child of the most High God.

In declaring God's blessings upon your life, you are killing the devil and putting him under your feet.

"I may wish I had different calves and thighs and no knock knees. But I like who I am as a person. And because I believe there is much more to me than my looks other people believe it too" **Felicia P Fields.**

"The body you are born with sculpts your personality as intricately and definingly as any life experience. For nearly eighteen years, my six-feet-seven-inches-ness made me shy, exclusive, and vigilantly self-conscious... Twenty-five years later, I love being tall. What could be cooler? It's my pleasure to grab soup or cashews on high shelves for mothers in supermarkets. I like the fact that my kids won't ever lose me in a crowd." **Peter Smith, writer.**

"The best we can do is focus on what we have the power to improve in ourselves and when it comes to body- love the one you're with." **Sara Davidson, writer.**

On self acceptance

God wants you to live in freedom from competition with others. It's easy to go through life competing with everyone around us. One of the reasons we heed to negative self-talk or negative attacks from other people is because we are not fully satisfied with who we are and to whom we belong. When we see someone that's more talented, more beautiful, or has more gifts, instead of running our own race in life and being comfortable with ourselves, we often feel inferior and start thinking, "I've got to do something to catch up with them." We begin to compete and compare. But this is a never-ending cycle .There will always be someone in life that appears better than us. Learn to be the best "person" that you can be and celebrate what God has given you. Learn not to be jealous of others, instead, celebrate what is going on in their lives, and at the same time celebrate your uniqueness. If you desire to fulfill your God-given destiny and reach your full potential, learn to stay focused on who God has called you to be. As you do this, you'll not only enjoy your life more, but you'll become all that He's created you to be because you're focused on your own race.

If you try to be like someone else, who will want to be like you?

This may sound hard, but just by being aware of what is not right in your life is 98% of the battle won. Once you know what's wrong, you will instinctively figure out a way to deal with it. When you learn how to accept who you are and how God created you, and also acknowledge your mistakes, you gain a kind of paradise, because then whatever anyone thinks or says about you becomes their problem not yours. When people try to put labels on you, they will not stick because you know who you are and you can ignore them because you have prepared yourself and know to whom you belong. Don't try to be anyone else but yourself, and in regards to the many false labels people try to stick you with, let those roll off of you.

I remember turning on the television and hearing the breaking news about a young aspiring musician from the UK who had died from a butt implant. After hearing this on the news, I also found it on the internet with the girl's pictures and information about her background. She was from a very well to do Nigerian family and was very beautiful. But she might have been caught up with showbiz and the media. In almost every magazine we pick up there are images of faces and bodies of people that are neither true nor realistic. This young girl looked good and had a nice figure but was probably told that in order to fit into showbiz she needed to have a body images look a certain way. She needed to fit in with everyone else.

Take
Away all the sparkle
All the glitter, gold and silver
And who is the person
You so admired and want to be like?

She also had friends who encouraged her because they too looked at these things the same way. During her passing in a hotel room in Pennsylvania, it was reported that she was with other friends who also came to the U.S to alter their physical images in order to fit in with the norms of that society. It was unfortunate that she died because of the procedures but this a good example for all of us to like the body we are in.

Friendship with you is all important because without it, one cannot be friends with anyone else in the world. **Eleanor Roosevelt.**

Whether we like it or not, we all have to accept and love the bodies we're in. Sure enough we can have all kinds of surgeries to have our bodies altered in different ways. But in a real world most of us do not have the money or the endurance to go through those numerous operations to achieve what the society and the media defines as a perfect body. Realistically, you can still go through all the operations in the world and still not feel satisfied with your looks and have to deal with what it will bring you the rest of your life.

When I had my baby, I really did not have any problem with weight. But to my greatest surprise, when I turned 30, things started changing. I realized that losing weight was very difficult. I did every diet and joined the gym but no matter what I did my stomach was just there looking at me. There were times I would get really frustrated because I was not able to fit into my nice jeans any more. But as I became older I learned that our bodies naturally change with time. This is because our bodies will never be perfect. They constantly change with our diets and age (hormonal changes) no matter what we do. I watched a documentary where one of the world's most gorgeous models said they too have issues with body image. They still think their butts are too big or their boobs too small. No human being is exempt from these sort of feelings.

But now I have come into my own, a new person that feels good about herself, and I really love this girl. I am more confident than I've ever been.

God wants us to help others win in life, to be people who reach back, invest ourselves in helping others become the best person they can be. We each have skills, influence, position and knowledge to impact to do just that. There are doors we can help open that can help launch them into their destiny. In the book of Act chapter 9:26-30 Barnabas was instrumental in helping Paul win at life. Whenever the disciples were apprehensive about Paul joining them in the ministry, Barnabas stood up for Paul, and in return, Paul was accepted. He went on to write several books of the New Testament.

Today, you can be a Barnabas in someone's life. You can help someone rise up and help them step into their God-given destiny. Simply look around. Who are you investing in? Who are you making better? Who are you helping up? Your destiny is tied to helping others. And remember, what you make happen for others, God will make happen for you! My brother was a Barnabas in my life. I want to, in turn, be a Barnabas in someone else's life. Who do you want to be a Barnabas to? Whose rope are you holding? Whose hands are you holding?

I realize I am a masterpiece handpicked by God. I will live with confidence, knowing that I am valuable in His eyes and have something great to offer my society.

God's Masterpiece.

God
Sees in us
A masterpiece
That one day will be done
His spirit works through all our life
To make us like his son

Ephesians 2:10 says that "We are God's masterpiece." That means you are not average. You are not ordinary. You are one of a kind. When God created you He went to great lengths to make you exactly the way He wanted. You didn't just happen to get your personality and traits. You didn't just accidentally get your nose, your skin color, your gifts or abilities. God designed you the way you are on purpose, for a purpose. The Apostle Paul said, "We should be to the praise of God's glory." In this passage, he's not talking about giving God praise with our words, although that is important. He's encouraging us to make our lives a living praise to Him! When you understand your value, and not only who you are but what you are, then your very existence will give God praise. When you are secured in whom God made you, and you go out each day being your very best, your life will give God praise! Honor God today by accepting who you are. Make the decision to be the best you can be. Get up every morning and set your mind in the right direction by making positive affirmations over your life: "I'm the apple of God's eye. I'm His masterpiece. His fingerprints are all over me." If you will learn to accept and approve yourself and have a right opinion about who you are then you're going to rise higher. God is going to pour out His blessings and you will live that life of victory that God has in store!

Start treating yourself as if you're the best thing that ever existed. In so doing, others will follow in your footsteps.

Always be a first-rate version of you than a second version of someone else. **From Sharon Witt's Teen Talk Series.**

It is true that there are friends, family members, husbands, or wives who want us to be certain ways. But you have to know that you are uniquely made and need to be yourself. Be happy with the body you are in. Be happy with who you are. You are specially made.

The media has played a very major role in constantly bombarding us with images, telling us how we should look. This makes us feel we have to be look-alikes of other people and not the original us. The question is, if you want so much to be an imitation of someone, who will be like you?

Trends and fashion may come today and tomorrow be gone. You don't have to follow everyone else's choices. By so doing you will just end up altering the original you who God made unique. How can this help you feel good about who God created?

Use your tongue to build up and encourage others, not destroy and sap out every self worth they ever had.

NO ONE IS PERFECT

Corinthians 12:9 says, "My grace is sufficient for you, for my power is made perfect in weakness." Do you feel weak or inadequate? Are you letting a weakness, failure or shortcoming keep you from letting God do great things in your life? If so, it's time to shake that off. We all have weaknesses and shortcomings. Every one of us has some unique flaws. In fact, the men and women that served God in the Bible doing extraordinary things were ordinary men and women with flaws, imperfections and weaknesses. But the key is they still were willing to serve God. They didn't let their limitations hold them back from serving God. And neither should you.

God wants to use you right now to do great things. If God chose us just based on our background, our past performances, even our talents or abilities, none of us may have a chance of serving. But God doesn't choose us because of what we are, He chooses us because of what we can become. And, as we serve Him we grow within our own self, developing a good self image. Don't sit on the sidelines of life anymore. God is saying, "I handpicked you not because you were perfect, not because you had it all together. I chose you because I can see the potential on the inside. I know what you can become, and He tells us, "Now you've got to get back in the race. Get your fire back. Get your dreams back. You're not supposed to sit on the sidelines until you're perfect. God wants to use you right now with your limitations. He wants to bless you in spite of your weaknesses. That way when you can grow to a new level, God will get all the credit.

Human beings are made in all shapes, colors, forms, etc. and that is why we have the too short, the too tall or the too fat. But you should not let those things decide how or when you serve God. Learn how to like and use your imperfections to help both yourself and others.

If you cannot fix it, flaunt it.

Be in control of what God has given you without heeding to any negative things you hear about yourself.

Confidence & self-esteem

Unfortunately, some people bully others to make themselves bigger but when they do that it is usually because they feel pretty awful about themselves in one way or the other. So they go around looking for who they could steal confidence from. A bully has no self confidence so they try to make others feel inferior in order to hide their own insecurities.

They do have one thing in common, putting you down.

Sadly enough, when you believe them, the bullying goes on and on. But if you don't believe their lies and look beyond what they are saying, the problem is 99.9% solved. So you have to stand tall and use your confidence and your self-esteem to push them away. When they see you are not going to be bullied they will go the other way.

Unfortunately we are living in a world where bullycide is becoming a talk of the day despite all the possible solutions people have come up with. Bullying can happen because victims lack confidence in themselves and they forget that

God created them and they are His children. Because of this lack of confidence and self-esteem they don't feel like they belong. It is our responsibility as a community, as individuals, and as parents to help people who are being bullied in any way to realize who they are and how important they are to us and society. They need to think positive about themselves and learn how to walk away from a bullying situation and report it to those in charge. We need to help them realize only the truth of who they really are.

Anyone can be bullied. It's happening everyday in our jobs, on public buses, in our homes, and on our street corners. But the group I have noticed that is so susceptible to bullying is teenagers. I believe this to be true because according to Erickson's theory, teenage years are a confusing time, where they are still trying to find a sense of belonging. They lack self esteem and when it comes to body image, this can be a very sensitive and serious area for many teens especially girls. Being a teen is tough because they have bodies that are constantly changing due to puberty and their natural developmental stages. While boys might find out their bodies are producing more sweat and odor, girls on the other hand might discover they have more curves and fat stores in places they never had. Because some teens don't know any better they get teased about their looks, their speech, their personalities, and they fall for it. Some kids or teens start cutting classes and some even drop out of school completely all because they can't stand being teased or called names. This bullying destroys their body image and self esteem and leads to depression which in turn leads to bullycides.

It is therefore the responsibility of a parent to help their teen through this challenging period so they could maintain a positive self image and esteem.

Teens need to be heard and not ignored. They need to feel they belong and not neglected.

There are a lot of magazines that exist and the media with images of what some of us and even our teens unfortunately wants to be like. Let's encourage them to read the right magazines not those that are focused on images that are not real. Let's help them focus on their strengths and improve on their weaknesses and strive towards greatness in their future. They are unique, they are God's masterpiece, and worth more than precious gold. They need to learn how to be themselves and not an imitation of someone else.

A very healthy self esteem is more like an armor against all the giants of the world. People who feel good about themselves are most likely to handle criticism and conflict well instead of falling for negative pressure. They are more optimistic and realistic. They have a good perception of who they are. They are motivated.

I mean that the only way you can come to feel worthy, and really good about yourself - the only way to find a life of meaning and joy - is to find your own voice, find your own path, follow your own heart and live your own life, not an imitation of somebody else's. **Maria Shriver**

Confidence allows us to face our challenges with boldness, honesty and courage. It enables us to live without fears or worries and to live real lives. We don't have to pretend we're somebody else when we are not. Confidence gives us the permission to be unique and different just the way God created us.

When you have a healthy self esteem or self image, you tend to be very confident and comfortable with yourself. You know what your strengths are and also understand that you are very unique and specially made.

On the other hand, when you have a low self esteem, it's very easy to spot you in a crowd. You tend to be a complainer, and blame everyone around you. You compare yourself to others and are never satisfied with yourself. Then you begin to slowly turn into a negative person, putting others down, and worst of all a jerk and a bully. You become the type of person that put you down originally.

The Blaming Game.

Unfortunately some people have made the big mistake of depending on others for happiness so when something goes wrong, they go through life blaming everyone else for the things that go wrong, giving your power to other people, which really does not help you get better. You can and should choose your reactions and learn how to take full responsibility for your actions. Situations caused by people do not just occur, but you need to learn how to cope with them. How we feel is a result of our choices and the consequences of our actions. But it's important to direct the blame away from others and take full responsibility for our own actions and responses.

Pain and suffering are inevitable but we have to learn how to manage our pain instead of letting it manage us. It's ok then to make a choice not to concern yourself with things you cannot change, and just focus on those you can! **From Sharon Witt's TeenTalk Series**

Applaud yourself even if no one else does.

There is only one you, so unique and beautiful. You may not look the way you wish you could, but you need to accept that. There is absolutely no perfect human being. When you get this concept, you will start to develop into a more lovable, peaceful and powerful person.

Developing a healthy self-image is the most important thing anyone should concentrate on because it helps you to achieve anything you set your mind on.

Unfortunately some people find pleasure in putting others down because it makes them feel bigger or better. But never let their words break you. You know the saying, "sticks and stones may break my bones but words will never harm me." Be like a rock and don't let your own tongue or other's tongues break you. Remember the tongue is as sharp as a sword, and there are people out there who are determined to suck out all of the good feelings you ever had about yourself if you let them.

Also remember that people can only put you down if you allow them to. If you choose to ignore and only listen to positive words people speak to you, then you retain your power. For every time you react negatively you give away a part of you. Ignore them, take your power back.

The most important word to use to fight the negativity from others or from within yourself is NO. When you say no to these two forces, you are letting them know that you will not let them affect you!

Words hurt and their effects can last a life time. Don't believe them but dare to believe God who created you .

Seeking help.

Everyone needs to be involved in the fight against bullying. Don't turn the other way if you see someone being bullied because that could be you or your family member. If it's more than you can handle, report it to someone else.

Looking the other way and ignoring a bullying situation is just as bad as being the bully yourself. So do something to stop it. Call for help.

Regardless of where we're from, we are one community on a narrow bridge. And wherever it leads, we're going there together. We thus have the power and ability to make the journey safe and enjoyable for all of us because there will be no need to hurt or cause pain for others.

I think now, more than ever, we need people with integrity, character and vision. We need people who want to lead, who want to encourage, who want to change the world and make it a more peaceful, hopeful and compassionate place. A place where people feel accepted and valued for who they are, who God made them to be.

The Word

While
Human beings
Cannot Always choose
Their situations or circumstances
Or what a split second can bring,
We can always choose our thoughts and actions.

"Real beauty isn't about symmetry or weight or make-up. It is about looking life right in the face and seeing all its magnificence reflected in your own." **Valerie Monroe-writer.**

I believe God made me exactly the way He wanted, and He equipped me with everything I need to live an abundant, fulfilled life.

I chose to live this day content, happy and grateful for what God has given me.

I will focus on what I have and not what I don't have. I will dwell on what is right in my life and magnify the good.

It's not what you are that holds you back; but it's what you think you are not.

Your life may not be going exactly the way you wanted it but it's going exactly the way God planned it.

I'll trade all my pain; I'll trade all my shame I'll trade all my old labels, I'll trade all my past, I'll trade my sadness, I'll lay them down to the joy of the Lord. **Women of Faith**

A little spark of encouragement can ignite great joy to one's soul

Prayer

Lord,
I would be
To others a cheering
Ray of light, inspiring them
With courage to climb some new -found height
Amen!!!!!!!!!!!!!!!.

Story #3

Who You Are Matters

Pa Njiki and Pa Ngassa's Story

"Who you are matters so make your life count", my father said at one of his sermons. He is a pastor and preached the Good News to thousands of people in many small villages in the North West province of Cameroon. A few months before his retirement as a pastor from his last congregation in the village of Bawock, he did something very remarkable. He took time to cut very little square cards from cardboard and painted them with different colors. He gave my siblings and I about a hundred of these cards each to print the statement, "Who You Are Makes a Difference." We finished approximately two thousand cards. None of us knew what he wanted to do with the cards except him. On one of the Sunday services after all the worshipers had entered the church and had sat in their seats, he called all of the church elders to stand in front of the congregation. During this very solemn ceremony my father thanked each of the elders for serving God and the Christian community with him so faithfully. He proceeded to ask their permission to honor and decorate each of them with a card. He used a safety pin to attach it on the jacket of each recipient and told them that, "Who they are makes a difference." After finishing with the Elders, he then gave each member of the congregation a card, and then he gave everyone two or three extra cards and asked them to go into the village and honor whoever they wish and tell them who they are makes a difference. But for the elders, he gave four cards to each and asked them to spread the good news to the whole community and to come back and relate their experiences the next week on how that kind of recognition impacted those people.

One of the elders went to his neighbor, Mr. Njiki, and honored him for helping his family get a piece of land to cultivate food. He gave him one of the cards, pinning it on his chest and telling him what a difference he has made in his life. Mr. Njiki was so proud to be honored of course. The elder then gave him the rest of the three cards and asked him to do the same to others he wished to honor, keeping the acknowledgment ceremony going throughout the community. The elder further told him that he needs to give a report on how things were going in a week's time. Mr. Njiki was not a Christian, he had never been to church nor did he have Christ in his life. He did not even want his family to go anywhere near a church house. His sons and daughters wanted to know who Christ was and would sneak out on special days like Christmas Eve, youth functions and Thanksgiving Day to attend church. Sometimes they would tell him lies just to come to church. Some of his daughters were in the CYF (Christian Youth Fellowship) but had to hide or lie to their father just to attend group meetings. Pa Njiki was a very proud man who did not like to honor anyone. Yet he wanted to be honored because of the village title he held as a sub chief. But after being honored by the church elder, he decided to do as he was instructed.

Later that day, Pa Njiki went to visit his friend, Pa Ngassa, who by the way was considered the most wicked, mean and grouchy person in the whole village. He sat with him for a drink of fresh palm wine and while they were drinking, chatting and having fun, Pa Njiki told the wicked guy how he admired him so much for being the strongest man in the village, and that he stopped by to honor him for that. This man was in shock but accepted the card which was pinned on his chest with a very bold smile on his face. "Nothing like this has ever happened to me," he said, this time with tears running down his chicks. Then, Pa Njiki further handed the rest of the cards to him and asked him to pass them on by honoring someone else. "The church elder who gave me the cards said we should come to church in a week with some feedback," Pa Njiki told him. He went on to say, "It is a recognition ceremony which is meant to let people know that they can make a difference and also see how these recognitions affect people's lives." When Pa Ngassa heard the words of the church elder, he became furious with his friend and said, "Njiki what has come over you? Even you too have joined those stupid church people with their lies? Take your card and leave my compound." But Pa Njiki was calm and told him, "My friend, if you will not take this from the church elder take it from me as a sign of respect. I have respected you all my life and didn't have a way of telling you. But when this idea of the recognition ceremony came knocking at my door, all

I could think about honoring was you. Please take it." While Pa Ngassa sat at his veranda murmuring and cursing church people, his friend Pa Njiki left and continued to wave him goodbye until he was gone.

That night, this mean guy, Pa Ngassa, thought about his seventeen year old daughter, so he went to his wives quarters, walked straight to his daughter's room and sat on her bed with the card in his hand. He said to the daughter, "Something very incredible happened to me today. Pa Njiki gave me this card pinned it on my jacket and told me he wanted to honor me for being the strongest man in the village. I was in shocked," he said. "But I am so glad Pa Njiki did that for me. He even gave me an extra card and asked me to find someone else to honor." As he left, I started thinking about who I would honor with this card. All I could think about was you. I want to honor you. My days are so busy and when I get home, I barely have time for you. Sometimes I yell at you for not getting good grades in school and have seldom appreciated things you do. I have not been a good father at all. But today I just want to let you know that you make a difference. You mean the whole world to me and I love you so dearly. Besides your mother, you are the most important person in my life. You are great, beautiful and smart and I love you. I wanted to sell you into an early marriage at twelve years old because that has been our culture. But when you and your mother refused, I hated you so much. I also did not like you going to that white man church and school. But I came to realize that a girl child deserves the same opportunity as boys. I was just ashamed and too proud to say sorry to you for all the hurt I have caused you. But right now, please find a place in your heart to forgive me. I love you and am so proud of you."

This girl, so startled, started sobbing and could not stop crying. With her whole body shaking, she looked up at her father and said through her tears, "Dad, earlier this afternoon, I sat in my room and wrote a letter to you and my mother and to everyone else explaining why I was going to kill myself, and ask for forgiveness. I was going to kill myself tonight. I didn't believe that you cared about me at all because of everything you have done to me from birth until this moment, saying mean things to me, putting me down with your words. You have never appreciated anything I did no matter how hard I tried. I just got tired of trying and living with such low self esteem all because of my own father. The letter is in my mother's bedroom underneath her pillow." Her father rushed to her mother's room and found a heartfelt letter full of pain, disgust, anguish, disappointment, self pity and hatred.

Meanwhile, the other elders continue on in their different ways to recognize people with the cards and telling them they made a difference. The story of these two people was the most talked about in the whole village. Pa Njiki and Pa Ngassa were the most feared, proud, arrogant and evil people in that little village. The last day of this ceremony was a Sunday and all the elders had to return to church and give their feedback. This was the most remarkable day in the life of that church and the village as a whole. The elders had asked all their friends and family members to cook and come to church with them on Sunday. Chairs had to be brought from a nearby school because there were many people who had come to witness this event. The church house was small and some people had to sit outside, thank God it was the dry season. These two people, Pa Njiki and

Pa Ngassa, came with all their friends and family members. Even the chief of the village came to church on that day. When it was time for the elders to tell the congregation how the recognition went, Pa Njiki and Pa Ngassa took over. They both thanked the elder who came to them. They also confessed their sins in front of the whole community and apologized as well to their families for all they did in the past. Most important was that both of them, in separate speeches, said they didn't know God but were ready right at that moment to know Him. Thus they both gave their lives to Christ. The day continued with celebrations that started after the church service. It was graced with eating, dancing and giving thanks to God. They continued the celebrations throughout the day in their homes with their families and villagers. From then on many souls were won for Christ. Many people got the message that who they are makes a difference and they could make their lives count for Christ.

This is a true life story that shook the whole community because this man Pa Ngassa was changed from that moment. He was no longer a mean, wicked and a grouchy man and made sure to let all of his children and employees know that they made a difference. He also made sure from then on he gave praises not only to his employees but his wife, his kids, and God. He created time out of his busy schedule to spend with family. He also attended church, confessed his sins, and testified to the whole community that God had changed him. Later that year he became one of the church elders. His daughter had a chance to live again instead of killing herself as she had planned. She excelled in school and her positive self esteem also increased each day. Today she is a medical doctor, married to another medical doctor and is an advocate for little girls in the village. She, along with her father, Pa Ngassa helped to encourage other parents in the village to send their daughters to school instead of entering into early marriages. They also supported others by paying their school fees. He helped several young people at his work place with career planning, and never hesitated to lend a helping hand when needed. He also never forgot to let them know that they made a difference in his life. People's lives in my community changed dramatically because of this event.

Who you are makes a difference despite any shortcoming you may think you have. Stop making excuses for yourself. The next time you feel like God cannot use you, just remember these famous people in the Bible...

Paul was too religious
Peter denied Jesus
Lazarus was dead
Timothy had an ulcer
Mary Magdalene was, well, you know
Martha worried about everything
Gideon was afraid
Moses had a stuttering problem
Samson had long hair and was a womanizer
Rehab was a prostitute
Jeremiah and Timothy were too young
David had an affair and was a murderer
Elijah was suicidal
Isaiah preached naked
Naomi was a widow
Job went bankrupt
John the Baptist ate bugs

The disciples fell asleep while praying
Jonah ran from God
Joseph was abused
Leah was ugly
Jacob was a liar and cheater
Isaac was a daydreamer
Abraham was too old
Noah was a drunkard.
The Samaritan woman was divorced, more than once.

YET GOD USED THEM. He can also use you to change someone else's life. He used my father through a sentence with simple cards he cut from a cardboard. "You don't have to be perfect to impact others," he said. There is no child of God who is perfect. He also added that no matter what you have been through, who you are is still important to God and to those you help. And if you do not complete those things that God assigned to you, that space will be left empty.

We always make one or two excuses for ourselves but this is a long list of people, famous people whom God used in one way or another despite their shortcomings. You can fulfill your potential for yourself or for God. Remember you aren't the message, but the messenger. If you have a message or a feeling that there is something you need to share with someone please do it, you can be God's helper. Sharing your life and your experiences with those in need can help. Don't let any personal shortcomings keep you from being God's messenger.

It is written in Proverbs chapter 18:4 that, "Your words are like life-giving water." Besides the Bible, did you know the only way God can use to bring healing and hope to others is through you and your words?

Everywhere we go there are people in need of life-giving water. They are lonely and hurting, they've been through disappointments and suffered heartache and pain. God has given us something to offer them - our words and our love. With these two things, we can bring healing. With our words, we can lift others out of depression. We can help set people free from the strongholds that are keeping them back. With our love we can give them hope.

God
Can take a
Lowly vessel, Shape it
With his mighty hand, fill it
With a matchless treasure, make it
Serve a purpose grand. God is looking for
Ordinary people to do extraordinary work.
God sees in us a masterpiece that one day will be done.
His spirit works through all of our lives to make us like his son.
Only God can transform a sin-stained soul into a masterpiece
of grace.

Words to Ponder

When you go through the day speaking encouragement, telling people what they can become or giving compliments and encouragements, you are living life as a healer. Your kind words are like pouring warm oil on the wounds. You may not know how you are helping, but God can take one compliment, one encouraging word, and use that to begin the healing process and set another person on a brand new course.

Be on the lookout for someone you can bless with your words. Call out the seeds of greatness in people. Be free with your compliments and encouragements because you're carrying life-giving water to those in need. Who knows, you could even be the spark that pushes others toward their divine destiny. Give others a push and help them win at life, because a little spark of encouragement can ignite a great endeavor. When you develop this habit of blessing people with your words, God will always bless you. When you help others raise their spirits, God will make sure to raise your spirits too..

Why not share this with a friend or two in the circle of God's love. Tell them they can make a difference to others so they have to make their lives count. They should create a legacy that will give meaning to their lives and to God. They should not belittle whatever contribution they make to their community and the world. You can't do everything and neither can I, but every one of us can do something good in this world.

You can do it; yes you can! Just make these promises to yourself.

I will not be consumed by my challenges; I will stay in the faith, focus on the good and keep the right perspective.

I believe God made me exactly the way He wanted, and He equipped me with everything I need to live an abundant, fulfilled life.

I will be faithful with the talent, time and opportunity God has given me and realize that when I make the most of it, God will

multiply it and give me more.
I will live with confidence, knowing that I am valuable in His eyes and have something great to offer my society.

A word of encouragement can make the difference between giving up and going on.

Whose "rope" is God encouraging you to hold?
When others help in times of need
We then should let them know
How much their strength has meant to us
To them our thanks we owe.

A Prayer

Lord, I would be to others
That life giving water,
Inspiring them with courage
To climb some new-found height
Amen.

Story #4

The gift of education AS A BOOSTER

Ramatu's Story

I met Ramatu one day while I was taking the train to New Jersey (USA). She too was going to Jersey and we stood at the same tiny corner because the train was overcrowded. We both recognized ourselves as coming from Africa, which sparked a friendship quickly. We started talking about our experiences in the U.S. and during our conversation Ramatu asked me where my stop was. I responded that I have never been to this place and was not sure so I was just going to listen to the train conductor to announce my stop. She asked me again what was I going to do there and I said I was going take an entrance exam into nursing school. We continued to talk but she soon got to her stop and had to leave. We exchanged phone numbers and kept in touch.

A few weeks later, she invited me to her home to help cook because she was having a party. I didn't have to drive because she was sending someone to pick me up. When a gentleman picked me up I realized he was driving me to one of the richest neighborhoods in New York. But I remained quiet just hoping that maybe we were just passing through this area. Soon, we arrived at one of the most beautiful homes I have ever seen in the U.S and Ramatu came out to welcome me. She told me this is where she lived with her husband and two children. Being in this area made me very uncomfortable which Ramatu noticed right away. She took my coat and my hand bag and told me to feel at home. She was so simple and had a very warm personality. She took me to the kitchen and asked me what I wanted to drink and if I wanted anything to eat. While we were waiting for her husband to bring some ingredients we had to use for cooking, she started talking about herself.

She said, "I will never forget the day I heard that a new government school would be opened in my village." Someone came to the house asking for any children who were not in school, and my grandma gave them my name. I was so happy thinking that I might get a chance to go to school. It was going to be a dream come true. I had only heard about school but never had the opportunity to get into one.

My grandma was getting me ready for marriage when I reached twelve years in accordance with the tradition of my community.

Like most ten year olds in my community, my life until this time had been divided between back-breaking work both on the farm and at home. I had brothers who were given more privileges than the girls. My mother passed away when she had me. I was told my father had beaten her so badly for giving birth to a girl. She got very sick from the beating and later died of her illness. I was supposed to be buried alive but my grandma sneaked out with me over night and ran to her home town. That was where I was raised, safe from death.

The idea of the school sparked yet another problem. Not everyone in the village was very happy about the white man bringing a school into the village. Some farmers complained that the school would deprive them of the cheap labor the children provided. Parents would lose the many cows and gifts they would receive when their girls were given to their husbands. Even my uncle wasn't in support of me going to school.

"What does a girl child need school for?" My uncle asked in anger. They are supposed to get married, bear children and work on the farm he added.

But fortunately for us, that was not the view of the local chief who had given the white man the land on which the school was to be built. The chief said he realized that educating a girl is even more important than a boy because he believed that a man could always support himself and a family, but a girl could not. If educated, a girl child would be able to provide for her own life.

Ramatu told me that she finally had the opportunity to go to school where she did so well. When she completed primary school, she was sent to college and her grandma worked on the farm tirelessly to make sure her fees were paid. When she graduated from college she was offered a scholarship to study in the .U.S.

I was able to get my medical degree and I am a doctor now. I graduated from Columbia University six years ago. This party I am having today is a send-off party for my family. We are going back to Africa. I want to open a school for girls and an orphanage for the forgotten children. I want to give them the same chance I was given. God spared my life for a reason and I believe this is why I must go home. This is my calling. It's all I want to do with my life.

It wouldn't be an exaggeration to say that through the achievements of my friend Ramatu, the eyes of a remote community have been opened onto the world.

I thought her story was so amazing and inspiring. I have read and heard stories of girls around the world like Ramatu who were once considered the forgotten, who had a second chance by means of education and have been impacting others around the world.

I believe that everyone, regardless of whatever they have been through deserve a second chance. It is also my belief that if you educate the girl child, you educate the family, the village, the community, the country and the world.

In my culture, when you have a child out of wedlock, you are almost considered the forgotten and in most cases you are the forgotten. You are considered second class or rejected cargo. You can never amount to anything. For many years I have wanted to go back and give that second chance to those who don't have anyone to give it to them.

Educating as many people as possible especially the girl child, remains the number one key to freedom. That freedom can raise your low self esteem, remove that humiliation, self-defeat and help get you out of poverty. Go to school and get a diploma and do not settle for anything less. You can still follow your heart and can still find the purpose for which you are here on earth. An education can help you achieve that goal. You can be a teenage/single mother but still be an outstanding woman. Do not listen to people who tell you things such as you cannot do it, never take no for an answer or settle for any less. I am writing from personal experience. I was a teen mother and even though from a continent with very little or no opportunities, I thrived because of an education.

Education is a human right with immense power of transformation.

Choose your friends from people who share your same goals. Those people who are ambitious and motivated to change their lives. Avoid negative people who tear down your self-worth. Stop making excuses for yourself.

Get some kind of professional training or learn a trade, grab any and every opportunity that comes your way if it's going to help you reclaim your life. When you are educated, no one can ever take that away from you.

It is a golden and everlasting treasure.

The Word

Do not only think of education as only a way to get a career to change your social and economic status but rather think of it in addition as a journey to discovering yourself, to discovering your own humility, what your contribution is to your community and to the world and also use it to expose yourself to the world. Do not belittle whatever contribution you have for your community or the world. **Ishmael Beah**

One's life has to be not only for you but for others. If your life is only for yourself, then it's not worth having it.

Because God has blessed me so richly and bountifully, I will always remember and serve the least of my brothers and sisters. I will live my life in such a way that every moment will be meaningful and glorify God.

A Prayer

Everlasting and merciful God
We pray for the lives of women
And children who maybe in bondage
Anywhere in the world. Help us to treat and see
Each other as your child. Open the eyes of people throughout
The world to see the education of a girl child not as a waste but as a
treasure. Keep all women and the "girl" child throughout
the universe in your love.

Amen

Story #5

Nkem's story

Nkem was a young man in his early twenties when I met him in nursing school. He was very quiet and intelligent, always making high grades. He also kept to himself most of the time. But being in the same class with him for a whole year, I learned a lot about him, more than he wanted me to. What I learned about him was fascinating. He was from East Africa. He was born to a single mother who was just fifteen at the time she got pregnant. He had explained to me that because of the culture from which he came, his mother had committed a very serious crime of having a child out of wedlock. It was considered a very serious thing in her village and she was isolated and treated as an outcast. He said her Grand Mother had told him that because of the stigma and all the ways his mother was treated, she became depressed and sick. Nkem was a premature baby who was born feet first and weighed approx 4lbs. In their culture, when a child is born feet first, he is called a witch or an obanjie which means he or she is of the devil. In their culture, that kind of child has to be killed and thrown away in a valley very far away from the village. The same treatment is used for people with other forms of disabilities too.

Fortunately for him, he was born into a Christian home whose beliefs were different from the culture of the village. So his life was spared because his grandfather was not going to allow him being killed. However, he was still treated as the obanjie and people, other than his family, would not hold him. Nkem grew up not knowing there was such thing as friends because of the brand that was put on him from birth. But he had a very wonderful Christian family who knew that he was not of the devil but a gift from God. They continued to take care of him and kept him in school.

Nkem was about 5 years old when his father came and took him and also gave him a very good education. While he was in his senior year in high school, his father died in a tragic accident. Now he had no father and a mother who was in a very far off country. He became very depressed being alone. However, he worked hard and received his GCE (the general certificate of education) certificate with good grades. In 2009, his mother successfully filed papers for him to come to the USA which thrilled them both. As soon as he got to the States, his grandmother on his mother's side registered him to start nursing school right away. It was while he was in nursing school that he learned from his obstetrics (OB) class that the reason he was born feet first was because he was in a breach position and not because he was possessed by the devil as his culture predicted. However, he had grown up not knowing the reason and also holding onto the fact that there was something wrong with him.

Limited by the system?

Do you ever feel like you are limited by the varied believes of this world? Do you ever feel like you are not worthy? Do people look at you as though you were an outcast? Maybe you have dreams and desires, but you don't feel like you have what it takes or the connections? Or maybe you don't have the right education. It's tempting to think, "I'll never rise any higher. Or I'll never amount to anything. I'm limited to the system that I'm in." But you have to remember, God likes to go outside the system! He likes to do unusual, extraordinary things. You may have a dream in your heart that's bigger than your finances. It's bigger than your education, bigger than anything that your family has ever done. And it's easy to think, "Well, I don't have the expertise. I don't have the connections. I don't have the right people behind me." It may seem bigger than it really is, but be encouraged today that you have God— you and God are a majority! Your dream is not dependent on other people. Who you are is not dependent on other people. God loves to take ordinary people and use them to do extraordinary things. You have not seen your best days yet. No matter where you are in life, no matter what environment you're in, no matter how impossible your dreams may seem, no matter what people call you, you need to know God already has a plan. He already has a way to fulfill that plan. If you will stay faithful God will go outside the system and take you places that you never thought possible! He will take you way beyond your dreams to help you live the life of victory He has in store for you!

All the things people said about Nkem and the way they acted towards him did him a great favor. He had no friends which meant his education was all he had to focus on, making him this very intelligent young man. People put labels on him such as obanjie and bastard, But God had a different plan for his life. He beat all the odds and the same people who called him those names are so ashamed they did. He is presently a nurse and has continued to excel. People don't determine our destiny, God does. But it had to start with us to wanting to fight and remove the stigmas and the labels people may try to stick on us. Learn how to look pass those imperfections knowing that there are many people in the world who wish they could just have a little of what you have. Be in control and use what God has given you without heeding to the negative things you hear about yourself. Who you are makes a big difference.

That means you are not average. You are not ordinary. You are one of a kind, very special and unique. When God created you He went to great lengths to make you exactly the way He wanted. You didn't just happen to be who you are. You didn't just accidentally get your nose, your skin color, your gifts or abilities. God designed you the way you are on purpose and for a purpose. We should be encouraged to give praise to Him who created us so beautifully! When you understand your value and that you are a child of God, then your very existence will give God praise. When you are secure in what gifts God gave you, and you go out each day being the best you can, your life will give God praise. Honor God today by accepting who you are. Make the decision to be the best you can be. Get up every morning and set your mind in the right direction by making positive affirmations over your life: "I'm blessed. I'm so specially made. His fingerprints are all over me." If you will learn to accept and approve who you are and have a good perspective about yourself then you're going to do great in this life. God is going to pour out His blessings and you will live that life of victory that God has in store!

The only way you can come to feel worthy and really good about yourself, the only way to find a life of meaning and joy, is to find your own voice, find your own path, find your own worth, follow your own heart, and live your own life, not an imitation of somebody else's or a life directed by what others think or call you.

This is because I have come to understand that first of all we are humans in our own right, thus entitled to our own lives, our own dreams, images, legacies and goals.

I think now, more than ever before, we need people with integrity, character and vision, people who want to lead, who want to encourage, who want to change the world and make it a more peaceful, hopeful and compassionate place. We need a place where more people feel accepted and valued for who they are. We need a world where we can all be ourselves and not an imitation of another.

The Word

Take
Time to be quiet
Hear what your own voice
Is telling you, listen and learn from it.
Learn who you are. Love what you have.

My mom said to me, MC (she always called me that), you have a choice. You can spend the rest of your life trying to measure up, trying to be like others trying to figure out and fulfill other people's expectations of you, or right now, you can make a decision to let all that go. Everything starts with you, by talking and advising yourself, by talking about what you know, what you feel and what you think. You can start talking about who you are to help others and the time is now.

I've learned we're all worthy of being loved and accepted just
for being ourselves.
So here is my question
And you ask it, too
Just who Am I?
Always remember
That who you will be is
Up to you.
Not your father, mother, brother, sister, husband—or me.

Take your time to consider and ponder on this.
Will you be a person
Who gives encouragements?
Or a person who sucks out
All the worth in another?
Will you be a person who puts a smile on another's face or
bring tears and sadness?
To make this crazy world
A far better place
To make some improvements
For our human race
We must learn how to let people
Be who they want to be, the "who" God created them to
be.

I have come into my own, into this new person - and I really love this girl. I'm more of myself than I've ever been...

Just who do you want to be?

A Prayer

God of mercy and kindness
Sometimes we forget your promises
And allow ourselves to become scared or jealous.
Thank you for enabling us to be a lead in the cycle of
God's love, in spreading your word—your truth to the
world
Amen!!!

Story #6

Tamika's story

Tamika was a woman I knew during my first year in the states. She was a single mom of four children, all from four different fathers. Yes, I know, and we all know it's wrong both for her and especially for the kids. She also knew that what she did was wrong. She was already ignored by her family and society. People called her useless and a waste, but even so, she was a fighter. She worked at two different stores in order to provide for her family instead of depending on public assistance, as it is the norm here for some girls who find themselves in the same situation as Tamika. Most of the friends she had were into drinking and drugs, and were hanging out on the streets. Her friends also had children and all depended on public assistance for survival. But one day to the surprise of some of her friends, she told them she was going to end the friendship she had with them and go to school. She did not like the life she was living. It was destroying her and the kids God has blessed her with.

These friends laughed and made fun of her because they could not imagine her going to school when she could barely feed her kids now. Despite having four kids with four different men, she had been raped several times in her early years. These rapes were kept secret because of fear. No one in her family was ever able to finish high school or get their GED's. She was determined to break that chain and get an education.

Every dream starts with a great dreamer and Tamika had a dream. She told her friends and family that she had wanted to become a judge. This idea brought more laughter from everyone because they did not believe she could possibly accomplish such a task.

To begin her dream, she started by finding information on how to get her general educational development (GED) . First, Tamika worked with some great people who directed her to a college called Lehman College where she could be tutored for free. Next, she registered for the classes to start the next semester. With four little children it was going to be tough. There was a daycare close to the school that could watch two of her children.

School days were busy. Tamika got up very early in the morning to get everyone ready for the day. She had to take two of the children to their school using the public bus system, then return home to get the other two ready and take them with her to the a daycare that was by the school. She then attended her classes. This routine continued for a whole year until she finally got her GED. She was so motivated after getting her diploma that she wanted to continue with her education. She applied to Lehman College and again was accepted. She also qualified for financial aid which was a blessing and a help. With the same routine, she continued her college education for years and graduated with a degree in social science. After getting her college degree, she then continued on to eventually become a lawyer, making her the first in her family to ever attain that level of education. Tamika achieved something no one in her family had ever done . She removed a label that had been stuck on her family from one generation to another and started an amazing legacy. She instilled hope into the lives of many girls around her, girls who thought the only answer to life was the drugs, the alcohol, and prostitution.

All her four kids had opportunities to get educations and have better lives because of their mother. The first son became a lawyer and opened a law office with his mother. The second a son, became a medical doctor, the third a nurse practitioner and the very last baby is still in college. Thanks to a mother who had the strength to ignore those around her who put her down and laughed at her dreams.

The Word

Whenever people push you to the side as a write-off, do not heed to that because God never thinks of anyone that way. And we should not either.

God's dream for us and His plan for our lives is much bigger and mightier that we can ever imagine.

We are all equipped with some amount of strength inside of us to achieve whatever we set our minds on. We just need to get out of our comfort zone and be go-getters.

In everything we do in life, there will always be discouragements along the way, either from friends or family members or just nay-Sayers. What do you do in times like that? Give-up? Be a quitter? Or stand firm, stand up tall and ask the supplier of all strength and courage for a little bit more to continue to the finish line?

A Prayer

Almighty and ever living God
Give me strength and help me to practice
Faith so I may overcome any fears and insecurities that
Keeps me from becoming what you want me to be. Direct
my foot-steps Oh God so I may walk in that path that leads
to everlasting life.
Amen!

Story #7

Amina's story

When Amina discovered she was pregnant, she was so devastated. With no one to turn to, she pours her heart to out in her diary, confiding her feelings of panic and self doubt, as well as the desperate hope that someday she could turn her life around.

After the baby was born, she faces the most agonizing question of all. Can she really raise the child by herself?

When Amina was a young little girl from the North African country of Sudan she came to live the United States with her mother. She was the first in a family of five kids raised by a single mother. Their father had died in the war in Sudan. She was so excited about being in the states, but started hanging out with the wrong group of girls. All they did was drink alcohol, and have sex with men for money, food, and abusing drugs. Her mother's efforts to get her away from this gang, was unsuccessful. She started cutting classes, and the school principal, the administrators and school counselors tried to advise her all to no avail.

She got pregnant within seven months of being with the gang, and did not even know who was responsible because she had so many sex partners and was not protecting herself. She was in shock after finding out about the pregnancy, and had no one to talk to. But all her so called friends in the gang wanted nothing to do with her and disappeared. Now she was alone.

What would mom do if I tell her? She asked herself many times. Will she cry, yell, send me out packing, or disown me? With all these questions in mind, she decided to keep it a secret from her mother. At this point, Amina was in a lot of emotional pain and really needed someone to talk to, but there was no one to go to. So she decided to write in her journal every morning when she woke up about her feelings. Even though she was raised as a Muslim, she was attending a catholic school. So besides writing in her journal, she started reading the Bible where she found a lot of comfort. She also focused on what was important to her and started going to school regularly. Because pregnancy can never be hidden in a calabash, very obvious signs of pregnancy started showing. Her mother was overwhelmed working two jobs in order to sustain her family and missed the obvious signs of her pregnancy. But Miss Lopez, her classroom teacher saw it and called her into a private meeting to ask her if she was indeed pregnant. The answer Amina gave at this time was no? But a few weeks later when there was no way to keep denying it, she went to Miss Lopez herself and told her she was five months pregnant. Amina asked Miss Lopez for the impossible, "Can you keep this a secret between us and not tell my mother or the school administration?" It was tough for Miss Lopez because it was her place to report such things to the administration and to the child's mother, yet she decided to go along with the secret.

Meanwhile some of those questionable friends from the gang suddenly came back and asked her to have an abortion or better still make arrangements to give the baby away for adoption. Amazingly, she told them she would not consider either option, and was bold enough to tell them to stay away from her, which was a very big issue because she was a member of their gang and must abide to their rules. She then went back to Miss Lopez and told her the gang she had been in was harassing her.

Amina felt desperate, she asked for the very impossible from Miss Lopez, to help take care of born child for her while she was in school. Miss Lopez was a mother of four grown children who were no longer living at home with her. She decided to call her daughters and seek their opinion. Luckily enough for Amina, the daughters told their mom she should help her.

Amina told Miss Lopez that she knew she has wrong on how she was handling the pregnancy, and especially keeping it from her mother. She was ready to right the wrongs. She soon had the baby without public assistance and Miss Lopez took him as planned. Why the mother still didn't know at point, was a puzzle. Amina got a job in a local grocery store so she could help Miss Lopez buying diapers and formula for the baby. Miss Lopez's family was so nice and they all supportive.

Her first dream came true when she finally graduated from high school and had her diploma. When it was time to go to college, she chose one that was far away from home so she could take her son with her. She was so grateful to the Lopez family for all that they had done for her and her son. Amina had planned to pick up the baby when she was leaving for college. But Miss Lopez had also become so attached to the child that she felt like a grandma. Miss Lopez said that she would continue taking care of the child until Amina completed college. Amina agreed to let Miss Lopez take care of her son, but was able to take him from time to time. With all the difficulties, she kept pushing forward and soon graduated from college with a scholarship to study law in one of American's best schools, Harvard law school. However, when she was to graduate from college, something remarkable happened. All the Lopez family was at the graduation ceremony with her son. Amina's mother even came with all her siblings and friends. Miss Lopez had completely forgotten that her son was still a secret from her mother and relatives, and she gave one of the most beautiful speeches at the graduation ceremonies and included everything Amina had gone through to get this far in life. She told everyone how proud she was of Amina's achievements. This was when Amina's mother found out about the baby and felt so sad that this secret was kept from her for so long. She cried, and cried but soon the tears turned into smiles. She now had her daughter back who was out of the gang and soon going to Harvard. But most important of all, she had a beautiful grandson.

While in law school, she met the love of her life and they got married soon after graduation. They are both practicing lawyers, plus Amina is a youth counselor in her community helping to get girls away from lives in gangs and into school.

This was one of the biggest accomplishments any person could dream of doing, taking her life back. She made it! When Amina was asked in an interview with a journalist about her accomplishments and overcoming all of the things that she had done, she said, you can look beyond the labels.

Yes, she messed up being in a gang, abusing drugs, and sleeping with men but she knew there was something better for her and her son. And she was very determined to cross that line.

I am so proud of Amina, I hope you can see what courage she had to make a good life for herself. There are lots of boys and girls, men and women out there who are lost in one way or the other. I hope you can look pass the labels, help yourself and in turn help others .

The word

Being a life changer does not need someone to be a billionaire but the heart to want to help someone.

Change just one soul and you change the world.

Life is tough, really tough! But if we are determined and take the bull by the horns, putting our grand creator first, we can conquer any challenges that come our way.

What matters in life is not the quantity of life we live but the quality of life we live.

A prayer

Oh! Great Lord,
That I may be a useful
Vessel, a smile giver, a bread basket
A rope holder, a hope giver and a life Changer
Amen!!

Story #8

Not losing Faith

Rema's story

When you are down to nothing, God is up to something said Rema who was married to her high school sweetheart. Together they had won the lottery to come to the United States from their home country of Nigeria. But little did they know what was coming their way. While they were living in the States, they encountered problems with her family and his family in Africa. When a man gets married to his wife in Africa, some cultures expect that by the first or second year they will start having children. However, Rema had not conceived in the first, the second or third year. And because of this, her family started being very concerned. Her mother summed up enough courage to ask her what was going on and Rema's response was, mama, we have been trying and nothing is happening. However, we will do our part and leave the rest to God. Later Rema's mother-in law who lived in a small village was very upset because of the same situation. She packed her bag and traveled to the city of Lagos where Rema's sister lived so they could call Rema and ask her why she had not started a family. Poor Rema respectfully told her mother-in law same thing she told her mother. But that was not enough for her mother-in law. Sisters and brothers from his family started attacking from all angles with derogatory words like she is barren, she is sterile, and had killed all the children she had in her womb when she was young through crude abortions. Some said she was a witch, while others said she was just a gold digger who was out to use their son and brother for his money. They even went as far as asking him to get rid of her and take a new wife. Through all this, Rema's husband stood so firm beside her.

Meanwhile back here in the United States, they kept trying and going from one doctor to the other. All the doctors said was that biologically there was absolutely nothing wrong with Rema, and they had done all they could but there was no problem with her. This went on and on for many years. All the attention was only on the woman, because in some African cultures it is believed that if a couple is not having a child, it is all the woman's fault. They never in any way look at the other side to check if there could be anything wrong with the man as well.

It was a kind of family where because of certain cultural beliefs the woman has no rights what so ever to question the man. So Rema suffered through this for so long because of that cultural belief. But one day she was courageous enough to take the matter to their pastor. When Rema told the pastor, he invited both of them to come in and talk about their problem. The pastor had proposed to both of them to check if there was anything wrong with her husband. After this meeting, they had a big fight because Rema's husband felt so disrespected and embarrassed. This was like a taboo because the man himself did not think there could be anything wrong with him. But when he finally decided to see a doctor, he found that he had a low sperm count, the main reason why they had not been able to conceive for ten years. He was so embarrassed and asked the doctor not to tell the Rema of the results. But the doctor told him it was not a big deal and that he must tell her because they came to him as a couple. He told the man that it was something that could be fixed easily so there was no need for any fears. The doctor arranged a meeting for the couple and told them what the problem was and Rema being the woman she is, remained calm and thanked the doctor. But she was curious where they had to go from there. The doctor asked them to schedule another day and come back to discuss the best plan that would be good for them.

When Rema told me her story, she said on their way home from the doctor's office that day, no one said a word. The silence had continued even when they got home and continued to the dinner table and into the night. Her husband was so ashamed, guilty and embarrassed about the whole ordeal. Rema felt that she had to break the silence to try to console him. She told her husband they both have to thank God that they finally knew what the problem had been instead of living in darkness as they have for the past ten years. The husband also had concerns that the wife might go announcing to people that he was the one with the issue and not her. There were also fears that he was going to lose his wife to another man.

But Rema was not that kind of person. She promised her husband to stand by him so they could win together. Meanwhile her husband apologized for all the years of cursing and for all the false labels his family members had stuck on her. They both stood by each other through all the tough times and had continued to pray endlessly for God to bless them with the fruit of the womb. Meanwhile, the doctor had prescribed some medication for him that would help boost his sperm count. They followed through with the treatment and in the twelveth year of their marriage, God answered their prayers by blessing them not with just one baby, but with a set of twins a boy and a girl. By the next year, she had another set of twin, two boys making a big family of four children. Rema ended up having one more child two years later giving this story a very happy ending.

The family was the most celebrated in their village for what God finally did for them. But what about all those derogatory labels that was stuck on her by everyone, especially her in-laws?

There is something I know for sure. People don't determine our destiny but God does have the final say.

She kept the right perspective by refusing to heed to what was said about her because she knew that God had a plan for her life. They both trusted God and stood firm for twelve years.

Rema stands as one woman in a thousand out there who have been called barren, sterile and so forth. But is that what God says about you? There are people all around you who try to completely rob you of any self worth you ever had. Don't let their poisonous and derogatory words (false labels) stick on you in any way. Let God your creator label you. We all face challenges, but it's not the size of the problem that's important, it's our perception of the problem. It is how big or small we make it in our minds. Are you facing a difficulty right now? Is something not going right? David said in Psalm 34:3, "Magnify the Lord with me." Instead of magnifying what you're facing, magnify God. Instead of focusing on the downs of life, focus on the ups and give praises to God. No matter how large an obstacle may be, God is much bigger than anything we may face! God did not breathe His life into us to just barely get by and go around intimidated by our dreams and convinced that the giants in our lives are too big. And there is nothing too big that the Creator of the universe cannot handle. All power and might is in His hand. Learn to keep the right perspective. When you talk about God's greatness, your problems become smaller, and you release your faith for God to go to work and fight your battles! Rema kept the right perspective which paid big time. Psalm 139:16 says, "...all the days ordained for me were written in your book before one of them came to be." This means that the God we serve is a strategic, detailed God who isn't vague or approximate. God has our lives orchestrated down to the very second, causing us to be at the right place at the right time so we can meet the right people that He ordained before the foundation of the world.

God has laid out an exact plan for our lives down to the smallest details. He knows the people you're going to need to fulfill your destiny and has it all figured out. The pastor was there with the doctor in Rema's case. That did not just happen. God made it so. Knowing this takes the weight off and you don't have to worry. You don't have to try and make things happen. God is in control.

As long as you stay faithful, God will have you at the right place at the right time, and He will bring the right people across your path. As you honor God with your life, His divine plan will unfold. The right people will show up. The right breaks will be there. You will walk into your moments of favor.

The Word

Your life may not be going exactly the way you wanted it but it's going exactly the way God planned it.

When it seems impossible and I don't see a way out, I will stay positive and hopeful, knowing that God's hands are never tied. With Him, impossibility is nothing.

I will not be discouraged by setbacks, failures or delays. But will know God is in control. He is fighting all my battles for me.

I recognize that even though challenges and difficulties seems like they're working against me, if I stand firm in faith, they will ultimately work for me.

When things are difficult and I am tempted to get discouraged, I will remember all the great things God has done in my life. When God is for us, no one can be against us.

So many people gain their sense of worth based on what others think of them. Do they like me? Do they approve of me? Do they think I'm important? Many people become something they are not because they think by conforming to the expectations of others they will get somewhere in their career or in life. It is very freeing when you realize that you don't need everyone's approval to get where you want to be in life and fulfill your God-given destiny. All you need is approval from Almighty God. It's time to live secure being the person God made you to be, not what someone else wants you to be. When you are secure in who God created you to be and confident enough in the destiny in front of you, then it doesn't matter what others say or do. Make pleasing the Lord your number one priority. Not only will you live life in more freedom and happiness, but you will become everything God created you to be.

Keep the right perspective, trust in your great creator and wait patiently for Him to act.

A prayer

*Lord that I may
Recognize you have the
Final say And keep the right perspective
That I may wait patiently for you to act because
Thou art my God forever.
Amen.*

Story #9

Stop dwelling on the past.

I will not live my life in regret, but will look beyond where I am now, seeing new possibilities, being open to new ideas and expecting great things in future.

A song from my mother's Christian Women Fellowship group says keep ploughing ahead and never look back for he who holds the plough and keeps looking back is not fit for the kingdom of God. My mother took quite a while trying to explain what the words meant, because it got to a point where I was not able to let go of the past. I held on to a lot of things which in turn held me back, thus making it hard for me to move on. When I had my son, people called me all kinds of names from outcast to loser. But as time unfolded and I became mentally mature, I realized it was a waste of my time dwelling on things long gone and done, which I cannot change. I also realized that whatever we said or did in the past is history which I consider a place of reference and never a place of residence and is not worth crying ourselves to sleep about. We could, instead, use those mistakes to help us address future issues so we don't make the same mistakes again.

> *What matters is not where we were yesterday and what we did but where we are going and what we will be doing.*

It's truly alright to forgive yourself, shake off the dust of bitterness from past hurts and move on. If we can get this mind-set, then it's ok to leave the rest to God. My father always said to let go of the past and let God take control, for He alone can take our messes and turn them into miracles. He further said if you let the things of the past over shadow your mind, you will miss out on the good things of life like tremendous opportunities, new hopes and new dreams that every new day brings. He always advised people to stop being so entrenched in the disappointments and mistakes of the past. Yes, people might have said a ton of negative things about you, but they don't determine your destiny, only God does.

> *Therefore,*
> *Let's choose*
> *Happiness as an attitude and*
> *Forgiveness as a journey to freedom,*
> *Free our hearts from hatred,*
> *Free our hearts from worries,*

> *I choose to live this day content, happy and grateful for what God has given me.*

The biggest issue in our lives does not necessarily come from the situation we face but from the way we think of them. We could choose to forever let the problems to rule our lives. We could take charge of our minds and direct our thoughts towards positive things and for solutions to grow. Dwelling on things that have long been gone is very unnecessary and time wasted.

In the course of our lives on earth, all sorts of things will happen to us and around us. That's part of the dynamics of life. What matters to our well-being is what we allow to happen. It is from our inner souls that our personal world evolves. Even if you are blessed with bounty, you will miss the joy of living if your mind is not focus.

Time after time, we are challenged to maintain our beliefs, establish a great relationship with ourselves and within our abilities to set things right. We have to choose the opportunity to grow when faced with difficulties rather than see it as a problem. In each of our lives, there are things that will throw us completely off balance if we're not in charge of our thinking, for instance there can be tough financial crisis, parenting under pressure, problems at work, teenage and single motherhood, being laid off work plus many other things. When this happens, we can lose sight of the ability to control our feelings and reactions, therefore driving us to act in very inappropriate ways which can worsen things instead.

There are people around us like family members, friends, co-workers who are just so manipulative and find pleasure in giving others hard times. They enjoy seeing others sad and miserable. Watch out for them and don't give them a chance to exercise their power over your life.

Guide your mind and put your life into the right perspective no matter what the circumstances. Instead of wasting precious time dwelling on the past or on things that will affect your mind negatively, look for reasons to be happy, things that are meaningful and rewarding, get involved in activities that you like. **MAKE YOURSELF USEFUL**.

The Word

Happiness is an attitude and a decision. We have the choice to spend the whole day in our beds recounting all the bad things that happens to us or get out of bed and start each day with a positive attitude, looking for opportunities to grow, and excel in whatever we do, while thanking God for the privilege of living.

I will not live my life in regret, but will look beyond where I am now, seeing new possibilities, being open to new ideas and expecting great things in future.

God does not bless ungratefulness, He blesses gratefulness. Remember we are all building our own homes. We can choose to spend all our time and lives dwelling on what we do not have or thanking and blessing God for what we have.

A Prayer

Lord of compassion
Guide me in life so that I should
Focus on what matters, rather than on
The matter of things in my life and in the world.
Amen!

Story #10

THE MAGGOT AND THE PALM TREE

A Story of Forgiveness

Refusing to forgive is like letting maggots eat you from the inside out. My family has an acre of palm nut trees from which we have made a living for many years. After a few years, some of trees were cut down. My uncle who lived on the farm usually made palm wine from the trees, very sweet and fresh. I also realized that the dried maggots we used to fry and eat with fufu were from inside of the palm tree and I marveled at it all. One day I decided to chop one of the trees open and see what was inside for myself, then I realized there were live maggots actually eating the tree from the inside. It always takes a very gradual process of deterioration and before you know it the tree turns to manure. This is what we do when we keep that grudge inside of us. A grudge is like a maggot, like acid that burns you up alive, eating you from the inside. When I learned of this process and knew the benefit of forgiveness, I decided I don't have any time or energy to be angry with anyone. Actually when you do forgive it does not mean the person that hurt you was right, it only makes you a free and happy person.

Another sad thing that can happen when we don't forgive is that we harbor all the anger and hatred and we end up taking it out on the people in our lives who had nothing to do with why we are angry. Dare to forgive and free yourself. Stop carrying poison with you. Forgiveness heals and stops hatred.

Forgiveness is something I consider a mental and or a spiritual process of ceasing to feel resentment, indignation or anger against another person and ceasing to demand punishment or restitution. This could be for a perceived offense, a difference of opinions, or mistakes made. However, many people agree forgiveness is considered one of the most difficult yet very important processes. The most rewarding feeling in the world is when we let go and forgive ourselves or someone. Let's take a scenario where someone hurts you real bad, but comes to you after a few days and ask you honestly for forgiveness. That person is eventually free from whatever the situation was and if you refuse to accept his or her apology, then you will be the one to suffer the grudge in your mind. But on the other hand if you are able to put that behind you, you will benefit the most. It is not worth bearing a grudge because all it does is makes you sick, so let go. Surrender all your issues to God and let Him fight your battles for you.

There is a story about two siblings who lived in the southern part of my country. Nuke, the older son was very intelligent and thus considered the best of the family while Nark, the younger one, was also smart in school but was always cutting classes and going to town using his school fees to play around with women. Nuke had an opportunity to travel abroad for school but when Nark heard about it, he sneaked into his brother's stuff, removed his visa and passport and burnt them to ashes. His brother not only missed his flight but the opportunity to utilize his scholarship. This was a family that barely survived. There were times the parents could not even afford their school fees. This act was so terrible to even think about forgetting or forgiving. But, Nuke forgave him with the blink of an eye not only because his brother apologized but because he wanted his soul to be at peace and free. Amazing isn't it. It was hard but worthy and very rewarding. There are billions of other very horrible acts that people do that hurts others, but holding onto it also holds you back. Let's all choose forgiveness as a journey towards freedom.

I was once good at keeping an account of every little thing anyone ever did to me that made me sad, and as a result, my life was a big mess. I isolated myself and developed a very defensive attitude that made people very uncomfortable around me. People always said to me, Hey Claire smile, it's not that bad. I didn't know how to smile if I was not happy on the inside. And my mother told me, "My daughter, you are destroying yourself. You have to learn how to let go of those little things that people do to you so you can focus on yourself and be happy." It was a very difficult learning process that took time but eventually I got it and my life has never been the same! I realized that when people do things to hurt you and you forgive them whether they ask or not, you benefit even more.

Find reasons to be grateful

Instead of sitting around and being consumed by what people think about you, find reasons to be grateful. Yes there are endless reasons. If you were challenged to make a list of all the good things in your life, then you will be overwhelmed at some of the things you have taken for granted. If you are able to wake up every day and be at peace, that's enough to be grateful and thankful for.

Stop making excuses for yourself.

STAYING ORGANIZED (no clutters)

You may be asking, what has staying organized got to do with me reclaiming my life?

How is it going to boost me up?

It works!

Staying organized in any aspect of one's life not only help you to stay focused but helps you thrive in any kind of crisis. There are two types of clutter, mental and physical clutter. My mother always told us, do not carry any junk from yesterday into another day. And, never let anyone's bad day be yours. As time unfolded and I became older, I started understanding what my mama meant. When you are that kind of person who bears grudges and never let them go, they affect your whole being, from how you talk, act, think and interact with people.

When mental clutter gets hold of you, it transcends to the outside, and, your outward appearance changes. You start blaming the people, circumstances and everything around you. It is ok to surrender everything to God because when you do, it's like leaving all your clutter behind and moving into a brand-new place.

God can take the old beaten up person you are and make you new. There is no need hiding all our messes from God when he already knows them. It is only when you fully let him into all parts of your heart that you can experience his cleansing power.

The Word

It's simple: when you haven't forgiven those who have hurt you, you turn your back against your future. When you do forgive you start walking forward. **Tyler Perry, Film director.**

God's forgiveness is the door to a new beginning.
We can see the setbacks in our lives removed when we are willing to frequently and quickly forgive.

A Prayer

Oh! Lord, That
I may have the strength to
Forgive and forget the wrongs
Done to me by others, just as Thou has
Mightily done for me.
Amen

Story #11

THE MANGO TREE

The Daughters of Mami Accra.

There was a woman called Mami Accra who had four very beautiful and smart daughters. She saw that when her beautiful girls had become of age for marriage they were so picky. They spent time in their room talking about the kind of guys that come their way, and none of them seemed qualified. Each man they met seemed to have some sort of problem. After eavesdropping on their conversation for a while, she decided to do something interesting. She sent them to go look at the mango tree which was on the hills at the outskirts of the village. But the smart thing she did was sending them at different seasons. The first two daughters went during the rainy season while the other two went during the dry season. When they all returned she called them together and asked each of them to describe what they experienced about the mango tree. The first daughter said, "Mama, the tree was short, ugly, bent and twisted." The second said, "Oh no I don't agree with you. It was covered with green buds and full of promise." The third did not agree with anyone of them but said, "Mama, it was laden with blossoms that smell so sweet and looked so beautiful and was the most graceful thing I have ever seen." The fourth daughter disagreeing with them all said, "It was ripe with yellow, red, orange and green fruits, and they were full of life and fulfilment." The mother was so amazed with each of their judgements and then told her daughters that they were all right.

Remember, they all went out during different seasons and only saw the tree during one of the two seasons. Then she told them that you can never judge a tree by its colour because of how it reacts to the various seasons and the weather conditions like drought, hurricanes, floods and of course, good weather conditions. So by seeing the tree in only one small time frame rather than throughout the entire season, you risk making false judgements about the life of the tree.

Humans are like the mango tree because they go through different seasons and experiences in their lifetime. But these seasons make them who they are, stronger, more resilient, able to withstand outside influences, etc. Thus, when you meet someone do not make a conclusion quickly about who they are, as you might be making a mistake. Also, do not let the pain of one season destroy the joy of the others. Difficult moments that we go through in our day to day lives do not mean that our future will be difficult but rather prepares us for better days. For example, a great number of men and women are scared to be in a relationship because of what had happened in the past in other relationships. However, no two people re-act the same to the same difficulties. Do not settle for less but persevere like the mango tree does through the harsh weather conditions. This will make you come out refined and pure as the adage says "Tough times do not last but tough people do." Keep your faith alive, keep working, keep trusting, and keep your head high, and life will get better. Do not be quick to jump to conclusions about people because the joy, peace, love, and problems of any person cannot be experienced without being with that person through all the seasons of their lives. The person you think is the worst person might turn out to be the best person you have ever met. When I got pregnant in my early teen years and had my son, I thought my world was finished, and did not understand I was at a cross road in my life. I knew I was already considered out of the normal for a girl in my society. I was called names like second hand and rejected cargo. It took me quite a while to become comfortable around boys. But after some years when I did decide to date again, I knew I was doing it just for the fun of it. I knew there was never going to be a serious relationship like marriage for me and the guys I dated. I knew that even if they loved me and wanted marriage, their parents and extended families would not let them.

So I held on so strong to my education because I knew, like my mother always told me, that my education would set me free. The men always came rushing but I continued to be scared. However, in 1994, a young, educated and handsome guy came for the holidays from the United Kingdom. He had also come home because his family wanted him to find a girl from the village and get married. One evening while I was rushing to the farm from school to help my mother carry food home, I met him sitting at the entrance to their compound. He said hello in our native language and I responded and kept going. After a few minutes I noticed him walking behind me. When he realized I had seen him behind me, he offered to help carry the bag of cassava stems I was carrying. He then introduced himself but never told me he was from Europe. But we could always tell anyway if someone had come in from the white man's country. He was radiant and glowing with handsomeness. He was tall, smooth, soft spoken, everything a woman desires in a man. For all I knew, he was in his last year of medical school. We started a relationship and it grew into the best relationship I ever had. We both longed for each other constantly. We loved each other so dearly. He followed me one day to the farm to help me carry a bag of food home. While at the farm, he noticed I was not as happy as I usually was around him. Finally he could no longer take it and he asked me why the sudden change. But I did not tell him anything, all I said was that I was fine. The next day he asked me again and he started getting depressed about my unhappiness. Finally, I opened up to him. I told him I loved him so much but there was no point in continuing the relationship because I would only be hurting myself. And he said, you speak in parables, please let me understand you. I told him I have a child and was not worthy to be his wife. When I said that, he was in the biggest shock of his life. And he asked, "What has having a child got to do with you being my wife? I will be taking both of you anyway. I was not going to take you and leave the child." I found then he really did not have a problem with my son, but I told him his parents and family members would certainly have a problem with that. He said a child is a blessing not a curse. I dared him to try and make his intentions known to his family anyway and see what their reaction was going to be. I have five very beautiful sisters in my family, so when he told his parents and mentioned my father's name as the father in -law, they were very happy at first, but the mother said, which of his daughters?

You may not believe this, but it's true and funny. At the mention of my name, his mother passed out and had to be taken to the hospital where she recovered. The next day, she swore that it was only over her dead body that her son would make that kind of mistake. When he asked his parents why the horrible reaction towards me, all they could say was that I had a child at home out of wedlock. The father even said, "She is a very good girl. I always see her going to the market or at the farm helping her mother. She is very quiet and well behaved too but the child she had at home spoiled everything." His aunties and sisters almost made a fool of him with laughter. They asked him, "So all man know say da girl Na second class, rejected cargo, ashaowo, except you Mister Johnny?" The family swore to him they would never let it happen because I was a misfit, a condemned person, and they were not giving their blessings if I was the only one he found in the village.

They went ahead and found different girls for him to make a choice from, but none of them worked for him. After all, he came back to me the next day crying and so depressed. He told me it was not worth it being in this village so he left before the day had ended and returned to the United Kingdom. A week later he called me and told me that for the first time he was going to disobey his parents. He wanted me to come to the UK to be with him. I told him, we come from a culture where respect for parents is very important so I could not do it. He finally graduated from Medical School and got married to a Russian without the consent of his parents and refused to ever go home to his family.

*In The "**Danger of a Single Story**" the author warns, "If we hear only a single story about another person or country, we risk a critical misunderstanding. What you may think you know about a person or people maybe a complete opposite of what truly is. It is usually the exact opposite of what you know. I encourage everyone to develop a habit of getting to know people by having a* *direct link to whatever you want to know through either experience or education." When we reject a single story, whenever we realize that there is never a single story about anyone, we regain a kind of paradise.* **Chimamanda Ngozi.**

The Bible also tells us in the book of Matthew chapter 7:1-2, "Don't criticize, and then you won't be criticized. For others will treat you as you treat them."

This was just a single season, just one story of my life. Yet it was the one big weapon people used against me for a long time. But what about who I am as a person? What about the rest of the seasons in my life? What about the precious little boy I brought into the world. Isn't he supposed to be a blessing?

It is a lesson to everyone not to be quick to judge someone based on just a single instance about that person. Then you miss out on the other seasons in the life of that person. Let's allow God to be our Judge.

The Word

Don't Let People label you,
Even if they do, don't let them stick,
If they stick, remove them,
Re-label yourself with new labels,
What God says about you.
God determines our destiny, not people!

A Prayer

Oh! That I may not be too quick to judge,
I 'm just as human, not free from mistakes
Oh! That I am not even near perfect, yet I'm quick
To point a finger at others Lord, forgive me when I judge
Amen.

Story #12

FALSE LABEL AS A MOUNTAIN

Everyone hits walls; walls exist to be taken down.

False labels are like mountains or walls or roadblocks. Acknowledge the obstacles without giving them the power to stop you from being who you are supposed to be. Rather learn how to overcome external and internal walls and troubleshoot problems without doing you any harm.

In life, people are constantly telling us what we can or cannot become and what we have or don't have. It's just like they're sticking a label on us: too short, too slow, too old, too many mistakes, not talented enough, will never amount to anything and so forth. These labels are not what God says about us. If we don't know any better, we will wear them like they're the truth, and it limits what God wants to do in our lives. But understand, people don't determine our destiny, God does.

I was a victim of pregnancy very early in my teen years. And given my cultural background I did not only commit an abomination but the biggest taboo of my life. Unfortunately for me, the people around me were not merciful. They called me an outcast, second class girl, pikin born pikin, a failure, and worst of all, they said I would never amount to anything. But thank God I had a very strong support system. My family was there for me and gave me a second chance by way of an education. A chance I viewed as golden.

Teenage girls continue to fall prey to teen pregnancies. And when this happens, they are immediately stuck with those derogatory labels. People, young and old, continue to drift through life without knowing why they were created because of wrong labels they have been forced to believe and live with.

If you're going to rise to the next level and become everything God has created you to be, remove every label that is holding you back. You are not the bad thing people label you. You are what God labels you.

God labels you, "chosen, forgiven, restored, redeemed, valuable, a masterpiece." When you remember what God says about you, those wrong labels will not be able to stick, and you will see God's victory in your life!

The truth is that all those false labels did not help my self esteem. Every time I heard those words, it reminded me of what I was not. I was not what society wanted, I was nothing. I let those labels stick to me and I became withdrawn, quiet and isolated all because I allowed it. One day, I did what I am asking everyone to do, I took those labels off. I realized that God made me the way I am for a purpose. I might have committed an abominable act but God still considers me worthy. I realized I was a masterpiece and not a mistake. I also realized I was not what people called me but what I answered to.

When you keep your mind focused on the things of God and what He says about you, you will wear His labels instead.

I want to encourage everyone not to sit around in self-pity but to do their own part and leave the rest to God.

False labels can easily make people depressed and defeated causing them to look on the other side of life. You might have made some wrong choices and have had some setbacks, but God is a God of second chances.

We have a choice and that is to learn how to get rid of those old labels which tells us we are washed up, not useful, condemned, and start wearing new labels knowing that Jesus came to lift the fallen and the broken hearted. Or, continue to sit around in self pity thinking you are washed up and have to sit on the side line of life.

> *But the one thing I know for sure is that God likes to take people that are nothing just like you and I and make something out of them.*

> *For I know the plans I have for you, says the Lord. They are plans for good and not evil, to give you a future and a hope. Jeremiah 29:11*

> *You are not what people say you are but what God say you are.*

I remember watching a talent show called the X Factor. It is a great show because compared to a similar show, American Idol, it does not set as many limits to who could audition or who wins. If you have the x-factor which is what they want, then you are in and have a chance to win. A beautiful young lady of approximately forty years old and a mother of two auditioned with a very touching story. She said all her life she wanted to sing but was told she was too old and didn't have what it took to be a singer. And because of all those words, she heeded to them and almost believed the people that were telling her that. She had lost faith in herself. Ten years later, she had two beautiful kids and turned forty-two but that dream kept coming back. She said all along she didn't want to die without fulfilling her dream as a singer. With the great opportunity from the creator of the X factor, she decided to give her dream a try. She was so emotional and could barely speak. But when she did open her mouth and started singing, her voice sounded as though it was a heavenly angel. She not only sang beautifully, but believed in herself. Everyone in the audience gave her a standing ovation. She had the x-factor and was selected to move to the next level. False labels are like huge giant walls standing in front of us, a stumbling block and a thorn in our side. It is destroying and damaging.

This lady trusted in herself and had confidence she could sing. She knew God had blessed her with a very beautiful gift and she was determined to use it.

She decided to take her life back from her name callers, and put them to shame by letting them know that other people do not determine our destiny but God does.

The Word

If you went to heaven tomorrow, would you be leaving a gift behind that you have not shared with the world? Are there things in your heart you're not pursuing because you're afraid, or you think you're too old, you're too busy, or don't have what it takes? Now is the time to get out of your comfort zone and pursue what God has given you on the inside. It's never too late to pursue what God has placed in your heart, to pursue new opportunities, explore new hobbies, break bad habits, or get rid of wrong mindsets. God will help you accomplish everything that He has placed in your heart! As you take these steps to live life to the fullest, the rest of your life can be the best of your life. Dare to trust God and take a bold step of faith.

Liaza was another girl who was a little on the heavy side and geeky. She was bullied all through her high school years. Surprisingly, she continued to feel the same way even throughout her first year in college and felt depressed from believing those that called her names. Those derogatory words stuck to her and she had no self-esteem or self-worth. Because of this, she had thought of taking her life many times because she had no friends in college. One day Liaza met a classmate while eating that was interested in her life. She asked Liaza why she did not mingle with others in college and Liaza told her that she was depressed. Her new friend told Liaza that she should talk with the school chaplain. Liaza did set up an appointment with the chaplain and told him why she was so depressed. She told him that she had been made fun of most of her life by classmates in high school and college. The chaplain encouraged her to get rid of those things that others had said about her. He told her she was a child of God and that she should let Him into her life. Over time, Liaza began to feel better about herself. She began to make new friends, friends in the church that were not mean nor demeaning to her. The way she was looking at her appearance and self esteem changed. She began to look at herself in a positive way and her grades became much better. Liaza sought help and had the courage to change.

If you try to be like someone else, who will want to be like you? When you have a healthy self esteem or self image, you tend to be very confident and comfortable with yourself. You know what your strengths are and also understand that you are very unique and specially made. You are God's masterpiece.

On the other hand, when you have a low self esteem, it's very easy to spot you in a crowd. You turn to be a complainer, and blame everyone around you. You compare. You want to be like Mary or Rose, never satisfied with yourself. Then you begin to slowly turn into a gossip, putting others down, being so negative and worst of all a jerk and a bully yourself.

Count Yourself as Blessed

I have personally had my own share of crisis, including personal setbacks, which made people look at me as an outcast. But at the same time I have been blessed in ways unimaginable. From being born into the world by my parents from having a healthy life through the years, to waking up to the light of a new day and breathing this fresh air, to having an abundance of food, clothes, being blessed with the fruits of the womb, for an education, a job, shelter, friends and most of all for living in the greatest country in the whole world where I am protected as a woman.

I will focus on what I have and not what I don't have. I will dwell on what is right in my life and magnify the good.

I come from a continent where the basic necessities of life such as food, shelter, health care, water, clothes are very hard to get. Women and children are raped, starved, beaten and killed every day and have no place to live but here I am with everything I would want in life. I see myself so blessed and thank God every day.

The Word

I will use all talents and skill, God has blessed me with to the best of my ability and will not let anyone put me down.

I will focus on what I believe in and trust in God rather than in man. I will always and forever give God praise for His endless blessings.

I will live my life with an attitude of faith and will not let anything put me down

Do not focus on all the negative things in your life. Focus on God, He is a specialist in the impossibilities, hence nothing is impossible for Him.

A prayer

Giving and generous God.
Thank you for the gift of live.
Thank you for the blessings that fill my life
Help me learn how to be generous and share
My blessings with others.
Amen

Story #13

Oh! Yes, the World Is Mind

Na Nah's story

Today, I stopped in the farmers market to buy some vegetables and the lady who sold it was so attractive. I talked with her and didn't even care if I was late for work or not. She sounded so nice and I wish I was like her.

And as I turn around to leave, she said, "Thank you, for you've been so nice and it is always nice talking to people like you."

She went on to say, "But you see I am blind. I can't even see the nice person that is talking to me."

I said, "God forgive me when I whine. I have eyes that see, the world is mine."

Later while jogging down the neighborhood, I saw a little girl I knew. She stood and watched her friends play jump rope, but the look on her face was not very pleasant.

I asked her, "Why don't you join them little girl?"

She looked the other way without a word.

I forgot she couldn't walk. She had both of her legs destroyed by leprosy.

Oh my God, forgive me when I whine.

I have two legs and can walk, the world is mine.

While on my way to school I met yet another very beautiful woman who looked so much like an intellectual. She was well dressed, holding a suitcase and sitting with her legs crossed and reading the paper. She had the most beautiful hair, her body was so toned, and everything she wore seemed to be very expensive.

Then I saw something on the paper I wanted to read, so I went closer to her but discovered that she held it upside down. And I wondered why? But I asked her anyway if I could just borrow the paper for a few minutes when she was finished with it. But she gave me the paper and told me to keep it.

When she noticed the surprised look on my face, she came closer to me and said, "Well I know you may be shocked, but I can't read. I was just showing off as other people do." For a moment I couldn't believe what she had just said. But I thought, Thank you Lord. I can read and I can write. Forgive me when I whine, the world is mine.

This is a lesson to everyone to learn how to be grateful and appreciate life and never wish you were someone else. Be grateful for the way you were created and thank God for every moment and for the gifts of life. You were specially made to be the way you are. Just learn how to like yourself, be proud of who you are and establish a good relationship as well with yourself because if you hate who you are or want to be like someone else, no one will see who you are.

I met Na Nah at a friend's baby shower. She was very beautiful and full of life. But as time unfolded and our friendship grew, I realized she was constantly trying to be someone else. She wanted to compete with all the girls around her, buy what they bought for their homes, dress with the same kind of clothes they had, do her hair similar to theirs and so forth. She wanted to be the best and to be the center of attraction everywhere she went. Not a bad idea though. I knew Na Nah, who I liked to hang out with was in great need of help because she was not living her own life. She wasted all of her time asking people where they bought that dress or where they got that hairdo she saw at the wedding yesterday. Yet she was never satisfied. I then thought what are friends for? Am I going to call myself a friend and yet sit back and continue to watch Na Nah go down a wrong path? It was a hard decision to confront her, because she was not the kind of person that accepts criticisms. She was a very defensive person and always takes whatever people say as being jealous of her.

One day I told her, why don't you come with me to the park today? It's so beautiful, come and let's take a walk. After walking around the park for about half an hour, we sat down to cool off. I was nervous but I had already decided that I was going to talk to her. Well, she is not going to beat me up anyway, I said to myself. So I started talking and said, "Well, I did not bring you here just to take a walk with me but to talk to you about something else. You are a very nice person with a very good heart and a very wonderful personality. But over the years I have watched you go down and down a wrong path. And now I can't take it anymore." Strange enough she was so quiet and ready to hear me.

Then I opened up to her about my story. For so many years of my life, I wasted it trying to walk in other peoples shoes. I tried to be like them, act like them and look like them. I also let lots of negative things people said about me rule the way I felt. After all those years of frustration, misery and struggles I finally realized what a fool I was. I realized God designed me so special and wanted me to be just an original me. When I was pregnant with my baby, his father not only told me to lose weight but, to lose the weight so I could look like a certain other lady. And I said, "OMG! Are you OK? Do you realized am pregnant and that is why I have gained weight? Oh well, mister, there are many choices you can make. Be with me like this or go look for that ideal person with that ideal weight out there because I am not going to do that not for a million dollars. I have an unborn child inside of me and will not starve to death. But even if I was not pregnant, I would not lose the weight for you, but for me." The story of Na Nah and my story about my weight are examples of many young men and women out there who spend almost half of their lives trying to be like others. But the good news is that you don't have to compare or compete with anyone or anything. Our God expects us to be our very best the way he made us. My mother instilled this pride and very high self esteem in me. The hope and faith she instilled in me and what I later leaned about God in my life, made me feel better because I know He is there for me. Everyone is so uniquely made so be yourself and enjoy and give a banquet of praise to God for making you just the way you are. Be proud of who you are and walk with your head high because who you are makes a difference.

The Word

I have eyes and I can see,

The world is mine. I have two legs and can walk,

The world is mine Lord! Forgive me when I whine.

Forgive me when I am ungrateful. Never wish you were someone else but try to thank God and make better use of what He has blessed you with. Stop whining. Whining is ungratefulness.

A Prayer

That I can wake
Up to a bright and beautiful day
That I can breathe this fresh air
That I am in good health that I have two
Legs and can walk, that I have eyes and can see
That you have blessed me bountifully, forgive me
When I whine, the world is mine
Amen

Notes

Chapter 1 Story 1
Ephesians 2:10
Psalms 90:12
Proverb 11:24&25
Malachi 3:8
Lists—what is your purpose?
Rejected cargo—wasted
Second-hand girl—worthless.

Chapter 2 Story 2
1 Samuel chapter 16ff
Calabash—An African bowl
1 Samuel chapter 17ff
Act 9:26-30
Eph 2:10
1 Corinthians chapter 12:9

Chapter 3 Story 3
Proverbs18:4

Chapter 5 Story 5
Obanjie—someone possessed with Demonic Spirit

Chapter 7 Story 7
Calabash—An African bowl
Chapter 11 Story 11
Jeremiah 29:11
Ashaowo—a prostitute
Pikin born pikin—A teenager who gave birth to a child.

Conclusion

REMEMBER: THIS IS UP TO YOU

So here is my question
And you ask it, too.

Do you want to sit on the other side of life and be consumed by bitterness?
Do you want to heed to all the negative things said about you?
Or do you want to shake it off and listen to what God has in store for you?

Always remember!

That who you will be and whose side you want to belong , will be up to you.
Not your father, mother, brother, sister, husband—or me.
Don't rush it but take your time,
Take time to be quiet,
And ponder on it.

Will you be a person
Who gives encouragements?
Or a person who sucks out
All the worth in another?

To make this crazy world
A far better place
To make some improvements
For our human race

We must learn how to like who and whose we are. We must learn how to celebrate our uniqueness.

If we like ourselves, others will follow.

Remember, God used His own very hands to create the very tall, very short, the very disabled, very beautiful, and the very ugly. And it is this mixture of the human race that makes the world what it is. A very unique world.

I've learned we're all worthy of being loved and accepted just for being ourselves.

But I have come to understand that first of all we are humans in our own right; thus entitled to our own lives, our own dreams, images, legacies and goals.

And for those whom all they do is try to use their words to destroy, why not use it to do just one nice thing for someone that will instead build them up.

If you cannot say something positive to someone, don't say anything at all.

And remember the golden rule: Do unto others what you would want them do unto you.

Use your tongue not as a destroyer but as a builder, not as a sorrow giver but as a smile giver. Don't dirty your hands, but keep them clean. Don't leave a legacy of someone who was known only for his poisonous words.

There are people today who were born normal but ended with some form of disability because of accidents. While there are a great deal of others who were born with disabilities. It is not their fault. They didn't ask for it. They are hurting already so don't add more salt to an existing wound.

Whose hands are you holding? Make it your responsibility to lift someone up instead of push them down

Praises for False Labels

Labels are needed to help us know what a particular thing is and that can be good, however when labels are attached to people to keep them from fulfilling their purpose that is when they become false. If you are feeling empty, hopeless, and lacking purpose read this wonderful book "False Labels: Don't Let People Label You" .You will not only be inspired, but you may become an inspiration to someone. Nothing is impossible for God.

Etta Graham-Mitchell,
BA, MsEd, CRC, Seminarian Student

Can you imagine that God made you as unique as you are for His glorification? That is the fundamental preoccupation in Marie Claire Kuja's False Labels. The book draws inspiration from the personal experiences of number of youths across the world who have realized that some of the labels given to them by society do not hinder them from achieving whatever goals they set for themselves.

Presented through narratives by those youths who each tell their stories, and reinforced with biblical allusions and quotations, as well as a prayer at the end of each story, the reader is held spellbound by the wonderful ideas and fascinating experiences. The reader is moved with pity or encouragement, as the case may be, when they identify with some of those generalized or specific experiences-lived not only by those who tell the stories but which may be a global reality. The book teaches one through the various stories to shun all forms of intimidation and frustration and to realize that one can transform stumbling blocks into stepping stones and to change all scars into stars. The most glaring example is the defeat of Goliath by David in the most amazing circumstances and against the background of all odds.

This book is a source of psychological empowerment for all oppressed people in general and those who suffer various forms of intimidation. This book will liberate millions of people across the world to recognize how unique they are as God's creation and to celebrate this uniqueness everywhere, every time.

ATUMO DANIEL ETOH
Teacher and Examiner,
Advanced Level Literature in English
G.B.H.S Mbengwi, North West Cameroon

Contemporarily, I find the book serving as an inspirational document for the youth of today (socially, spiritually and mentally).It's contents, if read in its entirety, would also provide encouragements as well as linkage to God for readers who might be caught in between problems and know not who to turn to for refuge. I can fore-see the book rising to becoming one of the "Best selling" Inspirational authored books and would without reservation, recommend it for the future readings of Christian Youth Students all over the world.

Jonas Attuh-Mensah, BS, MPA, Administrator MMG-West
Farms/Castle Hill & Member Deacon Board
Eastchester Presbyterian Church, Bronx

This book consists of 13 uplifting stories that depict different individuals' struggles to overcome adversities that they have encountered throughout their lives. The author strives to give the reader hope in overcoming obstacles that are put in their way by other people through bullying and verbally putting another person down. Also, the author strives to show that it is possible to overcome things such as poverty, racial stigmas and antiquated cultural beliefs that hold us back. Do not be afraid to have dreams and to do all you can to accomplish those dreams.

Terry Berogan, Editor

In this book you will learn how to:

1. Stop being at war with yourself.
2. Stop dwelling on the past and focus on the future.
3. Be thankful to God and celebrate your uniqueness
4. Embrace your own story joyfully, completely and with pride
5. Be an original of you instead of an imitation of someone else.
6. Stand up for your name-callers,[bullies] this time, a little differently.
7. Believe that God can use you right where you are, exactly the way you are.
8. Use your tongue to build and not destroy.
9. Use your one and only life to impact others.
10. Always leave by the words of the golden rule [Do unto others what you want them do unto you].

www.falselabelseries.com

CPSIA information can be obtained at www.ICGtesting.com
Printed in the USA
BVOW061916260312

286119BV00001B/4/P